architectural interiors

SPAS

SPAS
Copyright © 2007 Page One Publishing Private Limited
First published in Singapore by:
Page One Publishing Private Limited
20 Kaki Bukit View
Kaki Bukit Techpark II
Singapore 415956
Tel: (65) 6742-2088
Fax: (65) 6744-2088
enquiries@pageonegroup.com
www.pageonegroup.com   .

First published in the UK by
RotoVision SA
Route Suisse 9
CH-1295 Mies
Switzerland

RotoVision SA
Sales & Editorial Office
Sheridan House
114 Western Road
Hove BN3 1DD, UK
Tel: +44 (0)1273 727268
Fax: +44 (0)1273 727269
E-mail: sales@rotovision.com
Web: www.rotovision.com

10 9 8 7 6 5 4 3 2 1

Editorial Director: Kelley Cheng
Editor: Serena Narain
Designer: Frédéric Snauwaert, Waynne Fan

Editorial Coordination & Text (in alphabetical order)
Adeline Loh (Australia)
Ellen Nepilly (Japan)

ISBN: 978-2-88893-004-4

Printed and bound by:
SNP Leefung Printers (Shenzen) Co. Ltd.

architectural interiors

SPAS

RotoVision

contents

contents

introduction

The former world traveller who roamed the world for exotic destinations has now evolved into today's spa traveller, who goes globetrotting to seek out the ultimate sanctuary, where the body can be briefly free of modern stresses.

Spas are now the destination à la mode for couples – honeymooners or couples celebrating weddings or anniversaries – and other social groups – best friends or families on holidays. For these new spa travellers, the experience of a spa, its design, atmosphere, treatments and facilities remain their chief priorities, circumventing even usual concerns like price. Spas have never been more relevant or integral to our contemporary lifestyle.

Within Spas features a broad range of spa designs across the Asia-Pacific including Indonesia, the Philippines, Australia and Maldives, highlighting the details in interior design and spa aesthetics that remain pivotal to a spa's success. Rich images accompanied by insightful write-ups reveal the sophisticated approaches to spa design that have emerged to suit a broad palette of tastes, desires and demands, from inner city spas catering to busy urbanites to pristine resorts that whisk you away from the hustle and bustle in everyday living. *Within Spas* is an indispensable resource for anyone interested and involved in spa design, feeding that elusive search for the perfect balance of mind, body and spirit.

TIBETAN ESCAPE

Banyan Tree Spa

Ringha, China

Proudly braving the elements in Shangri-La – the spiritual land of the Tibetans, Banyan Tree Spa Ringha is housed in an authentic Tibetan farmhouse that has been refurbished to reflect a luxury sanctuary.

NAME OF SPA **BANYAN TREE SPA RINGHA, CHINA**
DESIGN FIRM **ARCHITRAVE DESIGN AND PLANNING**
IMAGES COURTESY OF **BANYAN TREE**
LOCATION **HONG PO VILLAGE, JIAN TANG TOWN,**
SHANGRI-LA COUNTY, DIQING TIBETEN AUTONOMOUS
PREFECTURE, YUNNAN PROVINCE 674400, CHINA
TEL **(86) 887 8288 822**
WEBSITE **WWW.BANYANTREESPA.COM/RINGHA**

At an altitude of 3,200 metres above sea level, Banyan Tree Spa Ringha provides the perfect respite for travellers to acclimatise with a selection of thoughtful and sophisticated spa treatments. Guests arrive at the distinct separate Banyan Tree Spa building to recline in the spacious communal lobby, surrounded by intricate carvings and handcrafted Tibetan artefacts.

The spa comprises six treatment rooms, of which there are two deluxe single rooms with shower facilities, two deluxe couple rooms with shower, steam, rainmist and bathtub facilities, and two couple rooms with sink amenities. Guests who wish to experience in-villa spa treatments may choose to do so in the Tibetan Spa Suite category of accommodation, which features a private spa treatment room ideal for couples.

Guests at Banyan Tree Spa Ringha are encouraged to experience the true spirit of Shangri-La through treatments inspired by local beliefs. The 150-minute Himalayan Bliss draws on a combination of Black Sesame Scrub, Gui Shi Hot Stones Massage and Rice Wine Bath, perfectly bringing the senses in tune with the landscape. Warm relief from the Black Sesame Scrub is intensified by the Gui Shi Hot Stones Massage, where warm river stones containing auspicious symbols of Tibetan Buddhism are applied onto skin. A blissful warm bath completes this rejuvenating package.

Within a year of opening, Banyan Tree Spa Ringha has achieved its first accolade, by being awarded a Best Spa Honourable Mention at the T+L Design Awards 2006, presented by *Travel+Leisure*. This award paid tribute to Banyan Tree's in-house architect and design division, which evolved the unique conservation technique of constructing Banyan Tree Ringha.

ORIENTAL RETREAT

CHI, the Spa

Pudong Shangri-La Shanghai, China

Upon entering CHI spa, there is a palpable sense of detachment from the outside world. Be it from the atmospheric lighting and warm colours that cast a mystical glow, the Chinese and Tibetan artefacts, or the spacious yet cocooning interiors, they all lend themselves to the unmistakable, inimitable experience that has become the signature of CHI.

NAME OF SPA CHI, THE SPA AT PUDONG SHANGRI-LA SHANGHAI, CHINA
DESIGN FIRM HIRSCH BEDNER ASSOCIATES
IMAGES COURTESY OF PUDONG SHANGRI-LA HOTEL
LOCATION 33 FU CHENG LU, PUDONG, SHANGHAI 200120, CHINA
TEL (86) 21 6882 8888
WEBSITE WWW.SHANGRI-LA.COM

Winner of the 2006 Baccarat AsiaSpa's Spa Interior Design of the Year Award, this 1,000-square-metre haven of tranquility features some of the largest and most luxurious private spa suites in the city, offering guests the ultimate in personal space and timelessness.

Like a secluded sanctuary inspired by the mystical legend of "Shangri-La" captured in James Hilton's book *Lost Horizon*, CHI is spread out over an entire floor in the new tower of Pudong Shangri-La Shanghai. Each spa experience takes place in one of nine private suites, featuring a "spa within a spa" concept complete with an affinity bath with colour therapy, herbal steam and shower, relaxation lounge and changing, toilet, vanity areas. In addition, there are two hydrotherapy suites.

One of the unifying design themes of CHI is the use of a teak sliding screen based on the traditional lattice work of the Himalayas. The sliding screens change the dynamic of the spa suites during the treatment journey when they are moved throughout the space to manipulate the mood and ambience.

The interior design accents include references from tribal embroidered garments and textiles, the mandala symbol, and Tibetan and Chinese antiques used throughout the spa.

At Pudong Shangri-La Shanghai, CHI features signature therapies like Chi Balance, Ying Yang Couple's Massage, Himalayan Healing Stone Massage and Mountain Tsampa Rub, which use indigenous ingredients and techniques drawn from the ancient healing practices of the Himalayan region. CHI also invites guests to indulge in memorable spa rituals lasting between two to five hours – guests can choose from the Enchanted Journey, Indulgence of Time or Paradise Found.

Forest Springs

Mission Hills Spa, Shenzhen

In the midst of a majestic nature park reserves, the largest golf clubhouse in the world is the location of a spa sanctuary of the same scale. Forest Springs, the spa at the Mission Hills Dongguan Clubhouse, is an all-encompassing escape set in the heart of a lush landscape with a panoramic view of a tranquil lake.

NAME OF SPA **FOREST SPRINGS, MISSION HILLS SPA, SHENZHEN**
DESIGN FIRM **PAL DESIGN CONSULTANTS, LTD**
IMAGES COURTESY OF **MISSION HILLS SPA**
LOCATION **MISSION HILLS DONNGUAN CLUBHOUSE, NO. 1 MISSION HILLS ROAD, SHENZHEN, CHINA**
TEL **(86) 769 8278 8888 EXT. 81800/81811**
WEBSITE **WWW.MISSIONHILLSGROUP.COM**

Measuring 3,200 square metres, the world-class spa features 38 treatment rooms for men and 27 for women with full water therapy facilities, and eight couple rooms with showers and Jacuzzi tubs.

Its extensive offerings include a foot reflexology centre, hair salon, nail spa, a Chinese healing therapy room, spa retail boutique and a pool area, providing a comprehensive health and wellness experience for all its guests.

Featuring a design concept that is a mix of traditional and contemporary, Forest Springs offers a menu that is a fusion of traditional Chinese therapies and classic European treatments, bringing together the best of Eastern and Western modalities to address the integration of body, mind and spirit.

The spa also hired an artist to create some handmade, one-of-a-kind artwork to add colour to the space. Soft earth tones are used throughout the spa for a soothing ambience, which guests enter via a cocooning tunnel that leads to the reception.

Signature treatments include Double Impact Massage that offers twice the relaxation with two therapists simultaneously giving the massage in synchronised movements, and the Oriental Massage that blends Eastern theories and Western techniques to create positive energy and relieve tiredness. Forest Springs features exclusive French Beauté Océane products for its spa treatments.

SPRING RETREAT

Spring Valley

Mission Hills Spa, Shenzhen

Spring Valley, the resort spa adjacent to the Mission Hills Country Club, is found in the Mission Hills Golf Club, which is accredited by the Guinness World Records as the World's Largest Golf Club. A sprawling 3,200-square-metre complex, the spa is part of an extensive integrated family resort offering leisure and sports, entertainment and catering facilities.

NAME OF SPA **SPRING VALLEY, MISSION HILLS SPA, SHENZHEN**
DESIGN FIRM **JOEY HO DESIGN LTD**
IMAGES COURTESY OF **MISSION HILLS SPA**
LOCATION **MISSION HILLS COUNTRY CLUB, NO. 1 MISSION HILLS ROAD, SHENZHEN, CHINA**
TEL **(86) 755 2802 0888**
WEBSITE **WWW.MISSIONHILLSGROUP.COM**

Spring Valley features a natural tropical spa environment located adjacent to the 80,000-square-metre Mission Hills Country Club. With a design concept that highlights the spa's prestigious comfort by the countryside, Spring Valley comprises ten treatment suites, five single suites and five hydrotheraphy suites complete with hydro massage bathtubs, dry flotation beds and Vichy showers.

All the spa suites come with their own private baths, showers, steam and changing areas. A pavilion on the rooftop has been designed to host private yoga or qi gong classes, while relaxing lounges with waterbeds offer a view of the greenery.

Over 60 massages, facials and body treatments are designed to bestow the ultimate luxury of health and wellness. This comprehensive array of treatments and beauty rituals has been created in collaboration with a team of experts from Asia and Europe, bringing together the best of Eastern and Western healing philosophies and practices.

Signature treatments include Algotherm Cares, featuring professional marine-based beauty brand Algotherm from France, complemented with the latest equipment and technology. Spring Valley also offers special spa treatments and health fitness programmes specially designed for teens aged 10 to 15, so parents and children can indulge in a healthy spa experience together.

TRANQUILITY ZONE

Quan Spa

Sanya Marriott Resort & Spa, China

The first Quan Spa opened by Marriott International, Quan Spa at Sanya Marriott Resort & Spa, China, is a tranquility zone where guests are taken on a relaxing sensory journey.

NAME OF SPA **QUAN SPA, SANYA MARRIOTT RESORT & SPA, CHINA**
DESIGN FIRM **SHANGHAI JAHWA LTD**
IMAGES COURTESY OF **MARRIOTT INTERNATIONAL INC**
LOCATION **YALONG BAY NATIONAL RESORT DISTRICT, SANYA 572000, HAINAN, CHINA**
TEL **(86) 898 8856 8888**
WEBSITE **WWW.MARRIOTT.COM/SYXMC**

The inspiration for the spa is drawn from the local culture, including its traditional healing and wellness rituals, and is delivered in a way that is still recognisable but effective. The name Quan means "source of water", be it a spring, fountain or spa. It is also synonymous with another Chinese character that means "total" and "wholeness". Hence the word Quan is auspicious in nature as it refers to a source that is ever flowing with all things good and pure.

Quan Spa at Sanya Marriott Resort & Spa borrows from its seaside location with the use of oversized replicas of cone shells neatly recessed into subtly lit alcoves, a colour palette that represents the beach and huge Chinese bowls filled with palms, which give a surreal effect with the burning incense at night.

Signature treatments at the spa include the Spice Body Wraps and Masks, which offer a potent Oriental full body experience for 55 minutes. Local Chinese spices and herbs that are purchased at apothecaries and market stalls in the local town of Sanya, and organic botanical extracts supplied by Jurlique are blended to give guests a full body exfoliation, and help to relieve a variety of concerns they may have.

Vichy Showers and Baths at Quan Sanya Marriott Resort & Spa all use Qi water. Qi water comes from the use of specially designed vivifiers that change the surface structure of water through the energy field that it creates, resulting in "energised" water that is more easily absorbed into the body, and healthier to bathe in and to drink. This in turn stimulates detoxification and the immune system, promotes healthy skin and improves metabolism and blood circulation, to name just a few benefits. At Quan Spa, highly trained therapists provide a full menu of traditional and innovative therapies at this luxurious spa, where guests are promised a total relaxing experience that refreshes both mind and body.

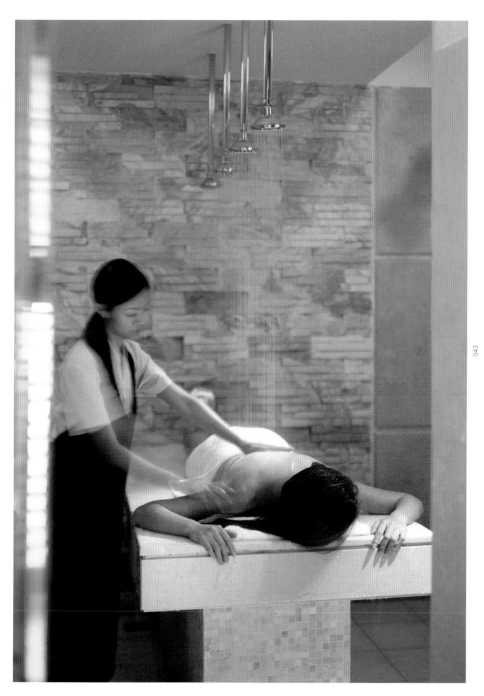

Plateau

Grand Hyatt, Hong Kong

A Hong Kong Spa with a difference, Plateau at the Grand Hyatt Hong Kong provides a resort spa experience in the heart of the city, with over 80,000 square feet dedicated to aesthetics, relaxation, fitness and culinary excellence.

NAME OF SPA PLATEAU, GRAND HYATT HONG KONG, CHINA
DESIGN FIRM MORFORD & COMPANY LTD
PHOTOGRAPHER VERA MERCER
LOCATION 1 HARBOUR ROAD, HONG KONG, CHINA
TEL (852) 2588 1234
WEBSITE WWW.PLATEAU.COM.HK

Plateau was conceived after the Grand Hyatt Hong Kong began development of a different concept at the 11th floor of the building, where the advantages of the large garden and guestroom area presented an opportunity to offer something new. Named after its location as a high, open and flat area, Plateau welcomes guests on the 11th floor with a reception area that sits adjacent to the fitness studios. Besides providing an extensive range of spa treatments, Plateau also features residential accommodation in 23 guestrooms and suites.

Designed by John Morford, who is also behind the acclaimed interior of Park Hyatt Tokyo, Plateau is a self-sufficient environment that ensures privacy and seclusion from the chaotic streets below. Just beyond the reception lobby is an expansive set of outdoor spaces. First up is a courtyard with lush plants and pool, beyond which lies the garden area that boasts of views of the harbour along one side. An integral part of the environment is a large number of specially-commissioned artworks. Emma Chen, a Hong Kong artist, created for Plateau a series of ceramic fish, frogs and turtles for exclusive use in the area.

The kernel of Plateau is the 14 rooms and suites, whose focus is a king-sized futon overlaid with luxurious Egyptian cotton duvet. This is where Plateau's skilled therapists apply their art, choreographing Thai, Swedish or Shiatsu massages to soothe and revitalise. The intricately minimalist décor is enhanced by hi-tech television and audio, and witty ceramic animal figures. A glassed-in oasis contains the oversized bath and rain shower, augmented by Aesop amenities from Australia, while solid double doors extinguish any sound of passing footsteps. The well-balanced décor and space in Plateau ensures that guests are in a state of calmness in preparation for the treatments ahead.

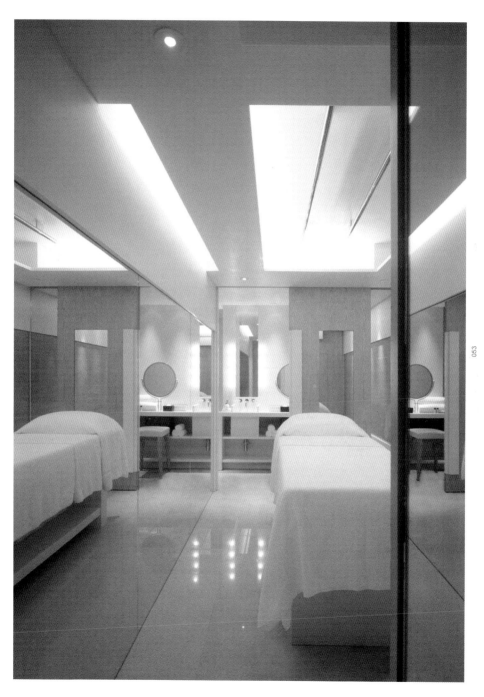

The Mandarin Spa

Mandarin Oriental, Hong Kong

Honouring the Chinese heritage and original design of the Mandarin Oriental, Hong Kong, the Mandarin Spa is a haven of tranquility within the heart of Central that combines harmonious design elements with therapeutic rituals.

NAME OF SPA **THE MANDARIN SPA, MANDARIN ORIENTAL, HONG KONG**
DESIGN FIRM **LIM, TEO & WILKES**
IMAGES COURTESY OF **MANDARIN ORIENTAL HONG KONG**
LOCATION **5 CONNAUGHT ROAD, CENTRAL, HONG KONG**
TEL **(852) 2522 0111**
WEBSITE **WWW.MANDARINORIENTAL.COM/HONGKONG**

The all-encompassing spa offers holistic rejuvenation and relaxation in a tranquil, meditative setting. Set in 2,100 square metres, the Mandarin Spa is positioned over three floors and incorporates an indoor swimming pool, fitness centre, holistic spa, Mandarin Salon and Mandarin Barber. The spa provides an ideal urban oasis for guests. Texture, light and space are integral components designed to stimulate the senses of the body and create a feeling of well-being. The mood is influenced by Shanghai in the 1930s – a bygone era of fantasy, luxury and comfort that is rich in culture and lends an air of opulence, warmth and sensuality.

Tactile materials including marble and dark wood veneers have been used throughout the spa. Each of the eight treatment rooms reflects its personal and absorbing sense of place, with sculptural features and a palette of lacquers, plasters and timbers, calming scents and lighting, as well as signature Mandarin Oriental touches.

Adopting a different approach to the traditional spa experience, the spa offers an array of innovative and restorative rituals inspired by both Traditional Chinese Medicine (TCM) and ayurvedic philosophies. The spa offers both individual and couple's suites, a Vichy shower, TCM consultations and Hong Kong's first ayurvedic sanctuary. The heat and water experiences have been created to soothe both mind and soul; guests can indulge in the ice fountain, Chinese herb steam rooms and experience showers as well as hydrotherapy in the unique Kneipp Pool, which uses a combination of massage pebbles and water to stimulate the feet and lower legs.

Highlights of the range of treatments available at the Oriental Spa include the Oriental Harmony, where two therapists work in unison with Mandarin Oriental signature oils to uplift and rejuvenate; and the Aroma Stone Body Massage, which is a blend of Native American Indian stones with specialised movements and techniques to create a sense of well-being and balance within the body.

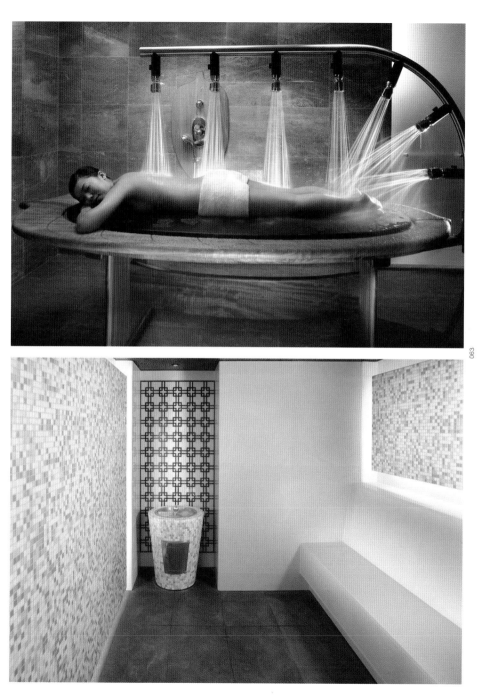

SPA ON A PENINSULA

The Lalu Spa

The Lalu, Taiwan

Resting in amidst the tranquil calm of the pristine Sun Moon Lake, The Lalu Spa has been designed as "an oasis for body, mind and spirit" and offers a seamless blend of professional service with natural luxury.

NAME OF SPA **THE LALU SPA, THE LALU, TAIWAN**
DESIGN FIRM **KERRY HILL ARCHITECTS**
IMAGES COURTESY OF **THE LALU**
LOCATION **NO. 142 JUNSHING ROAD, YUCHR SHIANG, NANTOU, TAIWAN 555, R.O.C.**
TEL **(886) 049 285 6888**
WEBSITE **WWW.THELALU.COM.TW**

Naming the architectural style of The Lalu Spa as an "ongoing style", the designer defines this as an ongoing style of moving forward – an ageless style that will remain fresh even after the years go by. Blending harmoniously into the local environment, building materials of The Lalu spa were obtained locally, promoting synthesis with the environmental setting.

The Lalu Spa features a total of 12 massage suites that include eight dual-purpose dry and wet massage suites (four single and four double suites), and four dry single massage suites. In the dual-purpose dry and wet massage suites, guests enjoy amazing lake views with a fireplace, an elegant double-sized bathtub, a stereo and a massage bed – making it an ideal haven for couples to retreat to.

The Lalu Spa provides an extensive range of body-soothing massages, purification treatments, rejuvenating facials and even the ayurvedic and chakra balancing treatments that are becoming popular. Guests can choose their spa treatments and one of four essential oils: Harmony, Passion, Purity or Balance. The Tiger Wind treatment soothes the emotions, re-energises the mind and body, and is most popular among men. The Joyful Expression treatment offers an herbal steam bath, followed by a soothing massage with a fragrant essential oil, and is most popular among women.

At the end of the massage, guests can take a steam bath, relax in the bathtub, and pamper their minds and bodies in the comfort of their spa suites, looking out at the lake and enjoying specially prepared drinks and healthy snacks.

TOUCH OF ZEN

Banyan Tree Spa

Phoenix Seagaia Resort, Japan

Banyan Tree Spa Phoenix Seagaia Resort, like each individual Banyan Tree Spa, has been designed to fit into its unique surroundings, using indigenous materials to showcase the culture and heritage of the unique architectural style and landscape.

NAME OF SPA **BANYAN TREE SPA PHOENIX SEAGAIA RESORT, JAPAN**
DESIGN FIRM **ARCHITRAVE DESIGN AND PLANNING**
IMAGES COURTESY OF **BANYAN TREE**
LOCATION **SHERATON GRANDE OCEAN RESORT, HAMAYAMA YAMAZAKI-CHO, MIYAZAKI-SHI MIYAZAKI, JAPAN 8808545**
TEL **(81) 9 8521 1351**
WEBSITE **WWW.BANYANTREESPA.COM/PHOENIXSEAGAIA**

Located at the 750-room Sheraton Grande Ocean Resort in the Miyazaki Prefecture, Kyushu, one of the spa's highlights is the "Banyan Tree Spa at Shosenkyu", which features three double-bedded garden Spa Pavilions situated next to natural hot springs (onsen) on the ground level, not only re-acquainting guests with the beauty and serenity of the natural world, but also making them more receptive to their senses. The architecture of the Spa Pavilions draws on local inspiration to blend seamlessly with the natural environment.

In addition, the spa features seven single and three double-bed rooms on the 39th floor of Sheraton Grande Hotel with panoramic views of the Pacific Ocean, vast farmland, world class golf courses and pine forests. For guests who wish to recreate the Banyan Tree experience at home, they can select signature aroma-therapy amenities at the Banyan Tree Gallery, which is located on the third floor of Sheraton Grande.

The spa menu offers treatments with a strong Japanese influence based on Banyan Tree Spa Academy recipes incorporating local ingredients such as pine tea, pine oil, apple and green tea, and seaweed. Speciality massages include Pine Delight and Miyazaki Melody – which are inspired by the surrounding pine forest and Shiatsu technique respectively. For a more indulgent session, guests can opt for one of the Five Elements treatment packages inspired by the Chinese philosophy of Five Elements, or the signature three-hour Royal Banyan and seven-hour Banyan Day spa packages.

TRANSCENDING TRADITION

Mandara Spa

Royal Park Shiodome Tower, Tokyo

Mandara Spa at Royal Park Shiodome is Mandara's first spa in Japan. Transcending the traditional and venerated concept of onsens, Mandara Spa offers a refreshing alternative in health and well-being.

NAME OF SPA **MANDARA SPA, ROYAL PARK SHIODOME TOWER, TOKYO, JAPAN**
DESIGN FIRM **KAJIMA DESIGN**
IMAGES COURTESY OF **MANDARA SPA**
LOCATION **6-3 HIGASHI-SHINBASHI 1-CHOME, MINATO-KU, TOKYO 1058333 JAPAN**
TEL **(81) 3 6253 1180**
WEBSITE **WWW.MANDARASPA.COM**

At Mandara Spa, Asian-inspired massages and body rituals combine with skin-boosting facials from French skincare specialist Decléor. Its hydrotherapy facilities merge the ancient Japanese traditions of bathing with the latest in modern equipment and technology.

Separated into male and female areas for comfort and privacy, the spa consists of eight treatment rooms in the ladies' area, including a Deluxe Spa Suite with private jet bath and shower. There are also three men's spa rooms, and separate men's and women's relaxation lounges. Here, guests are able to renew their energy in a hushed oasis that seems a world away from the pressures of urban life. Separate male and female hydrotherapy facilities offering Jet Bath, Super Jet Bath, Relaxation Bath, Silk Bath, Cool Bath, Steam Sauna and Dry Sauna are readily made available to guests.

Signature treatments of the spa include the Mandara massage, which is a not-to-be-missed unique blend of five massage styles – Japanese Shiatsu, Thai, Hawaiian Lomi Lomi, Swedish and Balinese – that employs two therapists working in harmony; the Warm Stone Massage, where the healing power of touch combines with the energy of the earth in a deeply relaxing massage; and the Ayurvedic Shiro Dhara, which is an ancient therapy that aims to calm the mind, balance the emotions, release toxins and encourage deep relaxation of the nervous system.

Guests can also shop at the retail boutique after their invigorating treatments. Products to enhance their spa treatments are available for purchase, ensuring their spa experience lasts beyond their stay at Mandara Spa.

A TRANQUIL ESCAPE

Mizuki Spa

Conrad Tokyo, Japan

Mizuki Spa at Conrad Tokyo features a modern Japanese design that evokes tranquility, while employing Western treatment methods exclusive to the Conrad Tokyo.

NAME OF SPA **MIZUKI SPA, CONRAD TOKYO, JAPAN**
DESIGN FIRM **TAKENAKA CONSTRUCTION**
PHOTOGRAPHER **ELLEN NEPILLY**
LOCATION **1-9-1, HIGASHI-SHINBASHI, MINATO-KU, TOKYO 1057337, JAPAN**
TEL **(81) 3 6388 8620**
WEBSITE **WWW.CONRADHOTELS1.HILTON.COM/EN/CH/HOME.DO**

Located on the 29th floor, the 15,000-square-foot Mizuki Spa is created with cypress, granite and soft lighting. Water and moon, two of nature's most powerful yet calming symbols, have been integrated into the design of the spa, which features several circular design elements all around. There is a relaxation room located in the centre of the spa with the hallway around it, made in such a way that people walk only in one direction around it, like a clockwork. Commanding impressive views from its high location, guests are treated to views of other skyscrapers of Shiodome.

The treatments available are a mix of modern Western and traditional Japanese styles. Guests should not leave without trying the harmonious spa's signature treatment that includes a royal beating with two bamboo batons. Using bamboo sticks, therapists lightly "drum" on the back of the guest to stimulate the meridians to unify spirit, mind and soul. Known for its strength and flexibility, the bamboo gently pummels the body during a 15-minute concerto. After which, guests can enjoy a deep soak in a traditional hinoki (cypress) tub, as well as an Essence Massage and express facial, and a deeply soothing cup of bitter Matcha tea during the 150-minute Muzuki Spirit Treatment.

The spa also includes a modern room with a Japanese style onsen bath included, which is made from Hinoki wood. The spa features flooring made of bamboo and wall panelling made from an African tree. Using grape seed aromatherapy from California's Napa Valley, as well as natural bio-cosmetics by German's Dr Spiller, the spa offers care treatment and essential techniques that relax the mind and body, harmonise the silhouette, revive the skin and generally preserve youth, making it a favourite of guests from all around the world.

ROYAL RETREAT

Kotoran Spa by Clarins

Kyoto Royal Hotel & Spa, Japan

Ishin Hotels Group's Kotoran Spa by Clarins is a total health and wellness facility combining traditional Japanese Zen simplicity and European elegance in the serenity of Kyoto, a city rooted in nature and history.

NAME OF SPA **KOTORAN SPA BY CLARINS, KYOTO ROYAL HOTEL & SPA, JAPAN**
DESIGN FIRM **W DESIGN INTERNATIONAL**
IMAGES COURTESY OF **KOTORAN SPA BY CLARINS**
LOCATION **SANJYO-AGARU KAWARAMACHI, NAKAGYO-KU, KYOTO 60580004, JAPAN**
TEL **(81) 7522 38489**
WEBSITE **WWW.KOTORANSPA.COM**

Asao Nakayama Wilson of W Design International designed the interior concept of Kotoran Spa by Clarins. It features a modern Japanese design with sleek lines, soft lighting, translucent natural tones and open spaces. The 652-square-metre spa has seven treatment suites, one of which features a deluxe en-suite Jacuzzi. Also located on the spa floor are four luxurious Kotoran guest suites where in-room spa treatments can be enjoyed.

Drawing inspiration from the rich traditions and breathtaking beauty of Kyoto, a city deeply rooted in history and natural abundance, Kotoran Spa by Clarins captivates all the senses. The use of water features, bamboo, stone, rice paper, Japanese stucco paint, luxurious fabrics and designer accessories all help to accentuate the relaxing ambience.

Beyond the physical elements, what sets the new spa apart is the treatments. Treatments begin with a personal consultation to understand each individual's skin and health needs. Guests then choose from a wide selection of aromatherapy, music, and lighting for a personalised qi experience.

Next, ancient Japanese meditation rituals are introduced while sipping on the spa's own signature mineral water, Kyo-no-Miyabisui, collected from the natural Kyoto spring beneath the hotel. The spa's signature treatments include the Bamboo Deep Tissue Treatment with Kotoran Meditation, which uses the techniques of traditional Asian massage that help to release tension from the body with deep strokes and firm pressure; and the Balancing Body Treatment with Kotoran Meditation, which guides guests to a total balance of their body, mind and spirit. Guests enjoy the Kotoran Meditation session with each of the two treatments. After each treatment, guests can unwind in the Relaxation Lounge. There is also a spa boutique where Kotoran Clarins products are available.

MODERN RETREAT

L'institut de Guerlain

The Shilla Seoul, Korea

The Shilla Seoul's L'institut de Guerlain Spa gives special attention to the small details that would delight even the most discerning spa connoisseur. The results are serene and spacious interiors and a muted palette of colours that include a tasteful mix of textures, elements and materials.

NAME OF SPA **L'INSTITUT DE GUERLAIN, THE SHILLA SEOUL, KOREA**
DESIGN FIRM **REMEDIOS SIEMBIEDA INC.**
IMAGES COURTESY OF **THE SHILLA SEOUL**
LOCATION **202 JANGCHUNGDONG 2-GA, JUNG-GU, SEOUL 100856, KOREA**
TEL **(82) 2 2230 1167**
WEBSITE **WWW.SHILLA.NET**

All materials are imported and the design team carefully selected the world's most comfortable and ergonomic equipment to deliver their programme of personalised treatment services. The spa provides special rooms for couples and suite rooms for VIPs. Especially in the Vichy Shower room, guests are treated to the highest quality personalised services, like hydrotherapy, which utilise world-leading Bouvier Hydrotherapy units.

The colour scheme is kept neutral to help create a soothing environment, ensuring guests are lulled into a tranquil state during their treatments. Treatment rooms also face picturesque views of the mountains, adding to that sense of peace.

Before starting any treatment, the guest is pampered with a 15-minute foot therapy. Temperature and lights can be set to induce the mood. Pine tree scent, soft music selected by experts in America from Bang & Olufsen audio, and flowers help setting the ambience to relax and enjoy the real spa.

The spa features ten treatment rooms, five foot-bath rooms, a Vichy shower room, beauty room, hydro-bath room and relaxing lounge. 32 different treatments for hand and foot care, body therapy and facial skin care are offered in the spa's extensive menu, all using Guerlain's exquisite body skincare and cosmetic product range. L'institut de Guerlain is a new generation spa that provides a unique East-meets-West experience in the most luxurious hotel in Seoul.

HUA HIN HIDEAWAY

Six Senses Spa

Evason Hua Hin Resort, Thailand

Nestled among 20 acres of lush gardens facing the Gulf of Siam is the Evason Hua Hin Resort, at the heart of which is the Six Senses Spa with a range of treatment rooms within and several outdoor champas set below the water level of the surrounding lotus pond.

NAME OF SPA SIX SENSES SPA, EVASON HUA HIN RESORT, THAILAND
DESIGN FIRM SIX SENSES RESORTS & SPAS
IMAGES COURTESY OF SIX SENSES RESORTS & SPAS
LOCATION 9 MOO 3 PAKNAMPRAN BEACH, PRANBURI, PRACHUAP KHIRI KHAN 77220, THAILAND
TEL (66) 3263 5111
WEBSITE WWW.SIXSENSES.COM

Evason Hua Hin Resort & Six Senses Spa has won accolades since it opened, including the *Conde Nast Traveler's* "World's Top 100 places to spend your special vacation" and the Conde Nast Reader's Travel Award 2005 for its excellent service. Positioned as one of the very top resorts in Asia, it is located at Pranburi, approximately 30 kilometres south of Hua Hin town and 230 kilometres from Bangkok, set amongst 20 acres of beautifully landscaped tropical gardens filled with lotus ponds and waterways, and facing the Gulf of Siam.

The luxuriously appointed spa is adjacent to the beach and sets new standards in spa design. There are five treatment salas each surrounded by relaxing water pools. Inside the spa, there are three treatment rooms for couples, three single rooms, two dry saunas and two steam rooms, with all facilities complemented by water features and lush vegetation. Six Senses Spa's design concept is "to encompass more thought to customer flow and appeal to as many senses as [they] can", hence greater emphasis is given to the size and privacy of the treatment rooms, and to areas of relaxation around the spa.

The comprehensive menu of therapies at the Six Senses Spa is primarily based on natural skin foods that are freshly blended for rejuvenating facial treatments, massage oils, body scrubs and wraps. There is also a complete menu of wellness sessions featuring Iyenya yoga, pranayama, pilates and tai chi. Water tai chi also available to loosen and nurture stressed bodies and souls.

HAVEN FOR THE SENSES

Mandara Spa

JW Marriott Phuket Resort & Spa

Mandara Spa at JW Marriott Phuket Resort & Spa offers a haven for guests to rest, relax and rejuvenate. The name Mandara refers to an ancient Sanskrit myth – the quest to discover the precious elixir of immortality and eternal youth, thus Mandara Spa is considered a sanctuary of nature, where the essential elements of life are cherished.

NAME OF SPA **MANDARA SPA, JW MARRIOTT PHUKET RESORT & SPA, THAILAND**
DESIGN FIRM **BENSLEY DESIGN STUDIOS**
IMAGES COURTESY OF **MARRIOTT INTERNATIONAL INC**
LOCATION **231 MOO 3, MAI KHAO, PHUKET, 83110, THAILAND**
TEL **(66) 7633 8000**
WEBSITE **WWW.MARRIOTT.COM**

The 1,593-square-metre spa complex includes 16 exceedingly spacious, private double treatment suites and a full service beauty salon. The spa interior focuses on the exotic beauty of Thai traditional architecture and artefacts subtly blending with the classic elegance of contemporary design, evoking a feeling of "spiritual tranquility and harmony" with nature.

Five of the suites feature black terrazzo flecked with mother of pearl décor. Floor-to-ceiling glass windows and doors let natural light in while relaxing the mind as you look out over the outdoor massage area with draped curtains, like a four poster bed on ground level, cooling ceiling fan overhead, and the tropical water garden that surrounds it, planted with tropical plants and papyrus. A little water fountain tinkles in the background beyond which the fabulous private herbal steam room (also black terrazzo) and romantic twin outdoor "bird cage" showers await.

The additional eleven treatment suites were added due to high demand. Behind copper-clad doors, terracotta walls are decorated with wooden lattice panels and floor-to-ceiling glass doors open onto a private outdoor garden with double cascade showers. These five suites have a shared steam room (one for men and one for women) and toilet facilities.

A range of heavenly treatments have been developed from ancient natural healing remedies as well as beauty and rejuvenation secrets of Asia. They are presented with nurturing mindfulness. The spa products, adapted from traditional beauty elixirs, capture the healing and nourishing essence of nature, using the finest and freshest ingredients, rich in nutrients and lusciously aromatic.

BEACH GETAWAY

Aman Spa

Amanpuri, Phuket

Set on the tropical island of Phuket and alongside Amanresort's flagship resort Amanpuri, Aman Spa is a holistic sanctuary where personalised treatment programmes reflect individual needs.

NAME OF SPA **AMAN SPA, AMANPURI, PHUKET, THAILAND**
DESIGNER **ED TUTTLE**
IMAGES COURTESY OF **AMANRESORTS**
LOCATION **PANSEA BEACH, PHUKET 8300, THAILAND**
TEL **(66) 7632 4333**
WEBSITE **WWW.AMANESORTS.COM**

Aman Spa consists of six spa treatment rooms that are light-filled and spacious. The design of the complex has been based on the architectural style of the Ayutthaya period. The designer spent a lot of time looking at the temple complexes and monuments, which he then extracted and simplified, getting the form down to what you can build today both economically and in terms of livability.

The site is a peninsula with a beautiful beach, giving the spa in the resort a complete privacy. Most of the existing trees have been kept to help promote that sense of privacy. The pavilions and villas are built on elevated column structures to protect the natural configuration of the land.

Each treatment room in Thai-style pavilions has its own bath, shower, private steam room, dressing area and an open-air sala for personal reflection. Aman Spa facilities include a traditional sauna, black granite steam room and a fountain terrace where health drinks are served.

The extensive spa menu includes a range of healing therapies as well as traditional treatments such as facials, massages, body wraps, scrubs and baths. Aman Spa products are prepared with essential oils derived from organically-grown plants, ensuring guests receive holistic treatments that leave them with a sense of well-being.

Trisara Spa

Phuket, Thailand

The Spa at Trisara offers a sanctuary for all that is best in life. Using only organic products, the spa experience can be enjoyed in the privacy and seclusion of the Pool Villas or in one of the spa's six magnificent ocean views treatment rooms.

NAME OF SPA **TRISARA SPA, PHUKET, THAILAND**
DESIGN FIRM **P49 DESIGN & ASSOCIATES CO**
IMAGES COURTESY OF **TRISARA**
LOCATION **60/1 MOO 6, SRISOONTHORN ROAD, CHERNGTALAY THALANG, PHUKET 83110, THAILAND**
TEL **(66) 76 3101 00**
WEBSITE **WWW.TRISARA.COM**

Trisara, which means "third garden in heaven" in a Sanskrit language, has become a landmark in Thailand since its opening. The resort, residential villas and spa sit within a tropical forest above a private bay, only 15 minutes from Phuket International Airport on the islands' quiet northwestern coastline.

It is on this sublime location that the Trisara Spa is found on. The 1,500-square-metre spa has also set benchmarks with six private treatment suites lined in raw silk. For guests who wish to have their treatments outdoors, sea-facing daybeds with adjacent steam showers and whirlpools are located among the calming tropical ponds and garden. Yoga and meditation are a specialty, with the seafront meditation sala a haven of tranquility on the water's edge.

All six treatment rooms come with fabulous sea views of the Andaman Sea and guests are treated with Trisara's own product line, which is 100 per cent organic. The carrier oils are pure jojoba and a choice of aromatic massage oils are offered prior to a treatment.

Not to be missed is the spa's signature Senses massage, which is performed by two therapists. Guests who prefer a gentle massage would appreciate the Lomi Lomi, a massage that is inspired by the Hawaiian dance. Guests are also served with a fruit platter and tangy ginger tea, encouraging them to linger by the lotus pond after their treatments.

Banyan Tree Spa

Phuket, Thailand

Award-winning Banyan Tree Spa Phuket comprises recreations of royal Thai salas in all their splendour and glory, where guests can enjoy an exoctic blend of massages and body treatments inspired by traditional Asian health and beauty remedies.

NAME OF SPA **BANYAN TREE SPA PHUKET, THAILAND**
DESIGN FIRM **ARCHITRAVE DESIGN AND PLANNING**
PHOTOGRAPHER **EDDIE BUAY**
LOCATION **33 MOO 4, SRISOONTHORN ROAD, CHERNGTALAY, AMPHUR TALANG, PHUKET 83110, THAILAND**
TEL **(66) 7632 4374**
WEBSITE **WWW.BANYANTREESPA.COM/PHUKET**

Voted "Best Oversea Spa", "Top Resort Spa in Asia and the Pacific" and "Top Hotel Spa in Asia" by readers of *Luxury Travel*, *Travel+Leisure* and *Conde Nast Traveller UK* respectively in recent years, Banyan Tree Spa Phuket must certainly provide a sublime environment for relaxation.

Exuding intimacy, luxury and romance, Banyan Tree Phuket is situated at the Bang Tao Bay on the north-western coast of Phuket Island and is the creation of Architrave Design and Planning, Banyan Tree's in-house design arm. Banyan Tree Spa Phuket is the pioneer of the tropical garden spa concept and design highlights include the Asian watercourts, which are found throughout the area, adding to the calm ambience and sense of tranquility in the resort. Banyan Tree Phuket's design concept reflects a contemporary Thai style and tropical living, with heavy usage of natural materials including wood, granite and marble. Complementing the concept are local artwork and fabric wood panels.

While soaking in the exquisite beauty of nature, guests recline on massage platforms draped in green and gold silk brocades, surrounded by walls adorned with stone sculptures of dancing Thai maidens and meditating Buddhas. Adding to the exclusivity is a private courtyard that is surrounded by a lily pond. For those who wish to be truly pampered, there are spa pool villas available, where the one bedroom is transformed into an exquisite spa pavilion for in-villa pampering.

With emphasis on a "high-touch, low-tech" approach, Banyan Tree Spa celebrates the human touch and use of natural and indigenous ingredients. With an emphasis on Eastern therapies and a non-clinical, holistic focus on spiritual, mental and physical harmony, the spa offers an exotic blend of massages and body treatments inspired by traditional Asian health and beauty remedies. From an extensive list of treatments available, guests are at liberty to choose their preferential therapy, be it hydrotherapy, massotherapy or European and Asian massages.

EXCLUSIVE SANCTUARY

Rayavadee Spa

Rayavadee Krabi, Thailand

Rayavadee Spa, the exclusive sanctuary at luxurious hideaway Rayavadee, Krabi, is located in a stunningly beautiful location – in the famous Krabi Marine National Park, surrounded by towering limestone cliffs soaring out of turquoise seas.

NAME OF SPA **RAYAVADEE SPA, RAYAVADEE KRABI, THAILAND**
DESIGN FIRM **NITTIPATARA YENSUP AND VICHADA PHONGSATHORN**
IMAGES COURTESY OF **RAYAVADEE**
LOCATION **214 MOO 2, TUMBON AO-NANG, AMPHUR MUAANG, KRABI 81000, THAILAND**
TEL **(66) 7562 0740**
WEBSITE **WWW.RAYAVADEE.COM**

With a total area of 550 square metres, Rayavadee Spa blends seamlessly into the tropical gardens of the resort. By drawing on the immediate environment for inspiration, the interior and exterior design explore the relationship between health and the balance of the five essential elements: water, earth, wind, fire and wood.

The result is a unique and very personal interpretation of the Asian tropical genre that is grounded in warm and inviting earth tones. Custom-made brass motifs and carefully selected contemporary Thai art and craft add subtle yet fascinating accents to the treatment suite interiors and public areas.

The spa offers seven large treatment suites; three singles and two doubles in addition to the two double suites specially designed for Thai massage. Each suite comes complete with its own private shower, toilet and changing area, with a sauna in the double treatment suites. It is also accredited by The Leading Hotels of the World as a Leading Spa, one of the few spas in Thailand to receive this coveted accreditation.

The award-winning spa offers a full range of therapeutic massages, scrubs, wraps, facials, baths and beauty treatments, each promising relaxation, vitality and true self-indulgence in a remote and rustic setting. At Rayavadee Spa, guests are assured of relaxing experiences that impart a deeper sense of well-being.

GARDEN IN HEAVEN

Devarana Spa

Dusit Thani Hotel, Bangkok

Inspired by the concept of the garden in heaven, Devarana Spa excites the senses and makes guests feel truly special. Luxurious pampering and healing treatments are offered in a soothing, stress-relieving environment.

NAME OF SPA **DEVARANA SPA, DUSIT THANI HOTEL, BANGKOK**
DESIGN FIRM **P INTERIOR AND ASSOCIATES**
PHOTOGRAPHY BY **WHITE POST GALLERY LIMITED PARTNERSHIP**
LOCATION **THE DUSIT THANI, 946 RAMA IV ROAD, BANGKOK 10500, THAILAND**
TEL **(66) 2636 3596**
WEBSITE **WWW.DEVARANASPA.COM**

Devarana Spa's contemporary Thai design and décor invites guests to transcend the everyday world and provides a relaxing and welcoming atmosphere in which to enjoy premium spa treatments with traditional Thai service and hospitality.

Ideally situated in the heart of Bangkok with a subway stop and a sky-train station just a few minutes away, Devarana Spa, at The Dusit Thani, takes its inspiration from the concept of a garden in heaven, described in ancient Thai literature as being located at heaven's gate, surrounded by gardens and ponds with a heavenly scent, nurturing environment, soft melodic music and glimmering silver and gold decor.

A sense of entering the heaven starts as soon as you walk up the wide staircase through the ancient Thai style gate. The centrepiece of the expansive reception area is a long reflective pond, lined with several canopied couches. Vibrant colours, luxurious textures, natural fabrics and state-of-the-art decorative materials were smartly blended to create the ambience of contemporary Thai elegance.

All 14 well-appointed treatment rooms and suites, arranged around an elegant swimming pool, softly splashing waterfalls and a lush tropical garden, provide luxurious comfort and privacy with double rooms available for those who wish to share their spa experience.

With an emphasis on pampering and wellness, East-meets-West Thai health and beauty practices have been sourced from age-old therapies and updated with modern knowledge to pamper and revitalise guests. Therapists at Devarana Spa expertly deliver a variety of treatments to provide guests a haven of relaxation and bliss. Choose from services, including massages, facials, body, water and beauty treatments as well as spa packages, using high quality natural products to polish, nourish and rejuvenate. Devarana Spa offers an atmosphere of ultimate relaxation in its very own healing garden of heaven.

CHI, the Spa

Shangri-La Hotel, Bangkok

CHI, the Spa at Shangri-La Hotel, Bangkok, embraces a holistic approach to physical and spiritual well-being in a soothing ambience that seeks its design inspiration from the Himalayan region.

NAME OF SPA CHI, THE SPA AT SHANGRI-LA HOTEL, BANGKOK
DESIGN FIRM JULIAN COOMBS ASSOCIATES
IMAGES COURTESY OF SHANGRI-LA HOTEL, BANGKOK
LOCATION 89 SOI WAT SUAN PLU, NEW ROAD, BANGRAK, BANGKOK 10500, THAILAND
TEL **(66) 2236 7777**
WEBSITE **WWW.SHANGRI-LA.COM/BANGKOK**

Envisioned as a sanctuary of tranquility that is inspired by the legend of "Shangri-La", this 1,000-square-metre spa features design overtones of the architectural principles of a Tibetan temple. While the spa utilises Himalayan artefacts and contemporary interpretations of traditional Tibetan works, it also highlights the Chinese principles of harmony and balance.

The spa also plays on lighting elements, giving off a more dramatic intensity past the corridor leading to the spa suites. With light shafts penetrating the screens and washing down stone walls, colours are rich and finishes are understated and simple.

Teak sliding screens, a signature design feature of CHI, are also found in each of the nine private spa suites where each spa experience takes place. Based on the traditional lattice work of the Himalayan region, the screens move throughout the space to orchestrate the ambience of the room.

Keeping in mind the virtues of the legendary Thai hospitality, the CHI experience is based on the ancient healing traditions and philosophies of China and the Himalayas. With an extensive menu that offers over 35 specialised body, water, massage and facial therapies, CHI's signature treatments are based on the five elements theory, in which metal, water, wood, fire and earth are in balance to harmonise with the positive yang and negative yin energy within the body.

Maya Spa

Kirimaya Golf Resort Spa, Bangkok

Maya Spa is located in a high-end nature retreat just two hours from Bangkok. Found in the first boutique luxury resort in Khao Yai, the UNESCO World Heritage, and nestled at the edge of the revered Khao Yai National Park, the Maya Spa experience includes a discovery of nature's gifts and wellness treatments.

NAME OF SPA **MAYA SPA, KIRIMAYA GOLF RESORT SPA, BANGKOK**
DESIGN FIRM **FEBRUAR IMAGE CO LTD**
IMAGES COURTESY OF **KIRIMAYA GOLF RESORT SPA**
LOCATION **1/3 MOO 6 THANARAT ROAD, MOO-SI, PAKCHONG, NAKORN RATCHASIMA 30130, THAILAND**
TEL **(66) 0 4442 6000**
WEBSITE **WWW.KIRIMAYA.COM**

Maya Spa combines natural beauty with the chic elegance of contemporary living. It is luxuriously spacious and features idyllic views, where interiors blend effortlessly a fusion of modern Asian touches with natural linens and earthy woods. Imagine a quiet haven of fresh innovative design where guests can rest easy amid understated luxury that embraces the natural world.

Located in the clubhouse of Kirimaya, the spa features three private massage pavilion suites with double massage areas, a spa pool and two steam rooms, two indoor Thai treatment rooms, two outdoor massage areas, a gym, a beauty salon and a Maya Spa Gallery.

At Maya Spa, guests can indulge in their desire to rejuvenate, beautify or just relax in an oasis of pampered bliss, with a full menu of spa treatments that promote an overall sense of physical and mental well-being. Signature treatments include the Khao Yai Therapy, where guests can indulge in four hours of head-to-toe body bliss; and the Guerlain Orchid Imperial Facial, which uses the first complete anti-ageing skincare with Imperial Orchid Molecular Extract, a flower with an extraordinary longevity for an exceptional anti-ageing efficacy. Guests leave the treatment room with their face shapes redefined, and wrinkles and fine lines smoothed.

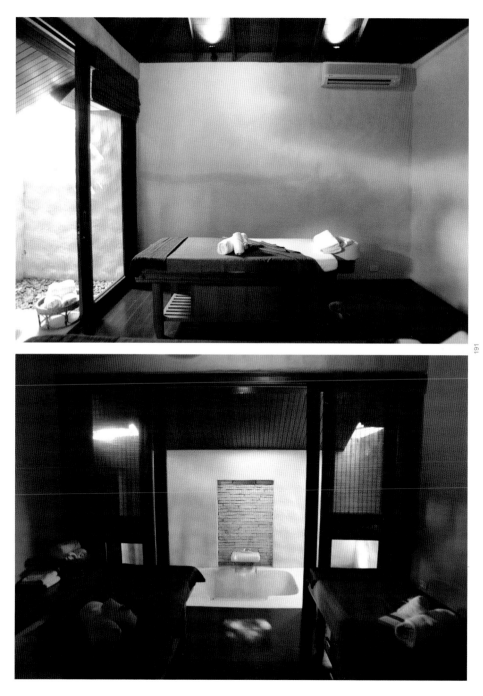

Dhara Spa and Ayurvedic Centre

Mandarin Oriental Dhara Dhevi, Chiang Mai

Nestled within the secluded grounds of Mandarin Oriental Dhara Devi, Chiang Mai, lies a hedonistic haven – Thailand's first world-class destination spa that is unique both in concept and architecture.

NAME OF SPA **DHARA SPA AND AYURVEDIC CENTRE, MANDARIN ORIENTAL DHARA DHEVI, CHIANG MAI**
DESIGNERS **MR LANFAA DEVAHASTIN, MR ANURAK KONGWONG, MR TEERAPOJ KAENCHANT &**
M.L. PRANGTIP PROMPOJ
IMAGES COURTESY OF **MANDARIN ORIENTAL DHARA DHEVI**
LOCATION **51/4 CHIANG MAI – SANKAMPAENG ROAD, MOO 1 T. TASALA A. MUANG, CHIANG MAI 50000, THAILAND**
TEL **(66) 5388 8888**
WEBSITE **WWW.MANDARINORIENTAL.COM/CHIANGMAI**

Taking up a palatial 3,100 square metres, the Dhara Spa and Ayurvedic Centre of Mandarin Oriental Dhara Dhevi is a sanctuary that seemingly floats on carved wooden balusters. A flight of white marble steps, flanked by white plaster banisters featuring leaf-like khanok – typical Lanna scrollwork – leads up to a restful spa lobby.

This magnificent palace-like teak structure, the colour of dark chocolate, stands in a grey granite courtyard overlooked by tall kapok trees. Every inch of the immense structure is embellished with ornate mouldings and sculptures depicting sacred animals or symbolic Buddhist motifs, loyally recreated by 150 Chiang Mai artisans from the original Burmese template in Mandalay, Myanmar.

The exterior is just as equally matched by the rich interiors where guests can enjoy impeccable service and a range of treatments drawn from three continents, with their origins spanning 4,000 years. From the lobby, a series of marble courtyards lead to the treatments rooms that are decorated with lavish Thai silk, polished teak wood and marble tiles. Adding to the décor are authentic Asian antiques. Here, 25 treatment rooms and suites have been designed for both individuals and couples as a refuge from urban stress and angst.

Among the spa's tranquil white marble courtyards and dark wood pavilions, guests are taken back to a time when ritual and ceremony were part of daily life. Every element of the spa draws its inspiration by life at a palace in the ancient Lanna kingdom, of which Chiang Mai was the royal capital.

Guests are also spoilt for choice with a broad variety of European, Asian and North African relaxation therapies, as well as Indian holistic treatments based on ayurveda, which means "science of life" in ancient Sanskrit. Among its numerous unique features are soothing Vichy showers, elegant hammams and giant rain showers beautifully appointed among the spa's dark wood panelled chambers.

SCENTS OF CAMBODIA

The Spa

Amansara, Siem Reap

The Spa at Amansara is conveniently located just ten minutes away from the vast archaeological park of Angkor, housed in a previous guest villa of King Norodum Sihanouk.

NAME OF SPA **THE SPA, AMANSARA, SIEM REAP, CAMBODIA**
DESIGN FIRM **KERRY HILL ARCHITECTS**
IMAGES COURTESY OF **AMANRESORTS**
LOCATION **ROAD TO ANGKOR, SIEM REAP, CAMBODIA**
TEL **(855) 6376 0333**
WEBSITE **WWW.ONEANDONLYRESORTS.COM**

The Spa at Amansara provides a well-earned respite after exploring the temples of Angkor and the sophisticated Khmer civilisation. Housed in a shaded wall compound and simple colour tones, The Spa at Amansara has the ambience of a gracious home.

Guests at The Spa can look forward to a range of massage and beauty treatments using Cambodian techniques and natural products. The Spa is accessed along a passageway that lies parallel to a long reflecting pool, which is set against a 43-metre sandstone relief. The four treatment rooms available all look into the reflecting pool. The reception area is accessed by steps that lead to the elevated area, which is bordered by a glassed-in courtyard lawn.

Soothing refloxology sessions and specialised treatments are available for temple-weary feet. Treatments utilise natural products and traditional Cambodian techniques. Signature treatments include the Scents of Cambodia, which utilises blended oils; Touch of the East, which is an oil-free stretch and acupressure release; and the Amansara Foot Cooler, which is a peppermint scrub and massage that will restore the spring in a guest's step. The latter is certainly one worth trying if they have climbed up the large number of temples at Angkor.

The Spa at Amansara aims to enhance a guest's mental and physical well-being. Treatments reflect holistic Khmer traditions and guests are comforted by the sanctuary-like feeling the spa evokes.

COME TO YOUR SENSES

Visaya Spa

FCC Angkor, Siem Reap

Set on the grounds of a former French ambassador's residence, now known as the FCC Angkor in Cambodia, and amidst the contemporary designer rooms, tropical gardens and saltwater pool, Visaya Spa adds a new dimension to the Angkorian bath experience.

NAME OF SPA **VISAYA SPA, FCC ANGKOR, SIEM REAP, CAMBODIA**
DESIGN FIRM **GFAB ARCHITECTS**
PHOTOGRAPHY BY **KELLEY CHENG**
LOCATION **POKAMBOR AVENUE, SIEM REAP, CAMBODIA**
TEL **(855) 6376 0814**
WEBSITE **WWW.FCCCAMBODIA.COM**

In Sanskrit, "Visaya" relates to the six senses. Visaya spa's pavilions and treatments are built around that concept, combining scientific and ancient knowledge systems to enliven its guests' senses, while restoring their natural beauty and balancing their energy.

Visaya Spa is nestled in FCC Angkor, which was built on the grounds of the old French ambassador's mansion, where towering trees rich and the sounds of nature creates an inviting tropical sojourn. Artistically decorated, the spa expresses a modern interpretation of the country's heritage, mixing clean lines with suffused lighting.

Warm yellow walls accented with splashes of orange and dark wood furniture set the tone for a soothing ambience, while indigenous artefacts are artfully placed all around the reception and treatment rooms for a local touch.

Visaya Spa features an extensive menu of aqua and aromatherapies, body massage and treatments, and face, hand and foot care. Guests can choose from concentrated 20-minute sessions to a luxurious four-hour extravaganza. Highly-trained and qualified therapists massage away guests' tensions as they indulge in homegrown spices and herbs blended to soothe away stress and promote holistic well-being. Each treatment at Visaya Spa has been designed to re-energise the senses of its guests and create an inner sense of wellness.

INDOCHINE ESCAPE

Spa Indochine

Hotel De La Paix, Siem Reap

Overlooking a swimming pool inspired by the ancient Khmer water gardens, the three-storey Spa Indochine offers a haven of peace and tranquility, where chic interiors and contemporary furnishings achieve a harmonious balance between modern design and traditional detailing.

NAME OF SPA **SPA INDOCHINE, HOTEL DE LA PAIX, SIEM REAP, CAMBODIA**
DESIGNER **BILL BENSLEY**
IMAGES COURTESY OF **HOTEL DE LA PAIX**
LOCATION **SIVUTHA BOULEVARD, SIEM REAP, CAMBODIA**
TEL **(855) 6396 6000**
WEBSITE **WWW.HOTELDELAPAIXANGKOR.COM**

In search of an exotic blend of spiritual and physical comforts, Spa Indochine has fused Asian and Western, traditional and contemporary arts to inspire a new experience where the greenery and breathtaking scenery of the environment create a quiet shelter, a retreat from the outside world. Spa Indochine envelops guests in a cocoon of calm serenity, with a new standard in beauty and relaxation, combining classical Asian traditions and current western spa products that draw upon age-old traditional ingredients.

Located in a hotel that is set with lush gardens and water features, Spa Indochine's art deco-inspired design is complemented by Khmer influences that embrace the future while respecting the past. Privacy is an ingredient in the traditional Asian lifestyle. Guests can also enjoy various treatments in their own Duplex Spa Suites, in-room massage facilities, rooftop terrace and plunge bath. A relaxing lounge that overlooks a swimming pool inspired by the ancient Khmer water gardens and the expansive rooftop relaxation terrace offer the ultimate in pampering and indulgence.

A sacred belief in the renewal of body and soul through healing human touch has long been essential to life in Southeast Asia. Spa Indochine incorporated these ancient massage traditions with essential oils, spices and aromas to smooth all the senses back to wellness. The Bantey Srei, a three-hour therapy incorporates a combination of body treatments, including a Flower foot scrub, Body Scrub and Wrap, 60-minute Body Massage and Herbal Elixir. Guests select their preferred body scrub, wrap and massage from the expansive Spa menu and the treatment begins with a pampering foot cleansing ritual, using an essential oil soaked with flowers, honey gel and scrub product. Spa Indochine's treatments have been specially designed and sought after for their soothing and restorative qualities.

SPRING REJUVENATION

Xuan Spa

Park Hyatt Saigon, Vietnam

Xuan Spa, which means "Spring" in Vietnamese, is located in Park Hyatt Saigon and features treatment rooms furnished with antique Vietnamese wood furnishings that reflect the elegant Indochine era.

NAME OF SPA **XUAN SPA, PARK HYATT SAIGON, VIETNAM**
DESIGN FIRMS **DAMANSARA ARCHITECTS AND EDC DESIGN**
PHOTOGRAPHER **PATRICK MESSINA**
LOCATION **2 LAM SON SQUARE, DISTRICT 1, HO CHI MINH CITY, VIETNAM**
TEL **(84) 8824 1234**
WEBSITE **WWW.SAIGON.PARK.HYATT.COM**

Located on the third floor of the hotel, Xuan Spa seamlessly combines the quaint feel of the city's French Colonial history with modern technology. The spa offers seven treatment rooms and one Vichy shower room, each with private showers and changing areas. Gilded mirrors and colonial wood cabinets also add to the Indochine design, which is emphasised by the Vichy shower that is incidentally the city's first.

Making it to the Hot List Spas 2006 by *Condé Nast Traveler*, Xuan Spa embraces sunlight, neutral-coloured walls and marble floors, complemented by facilities that are designed to reflect the beauty of the surrounding environment. It features a separate male and female wet area, including a Jacuzzi, steam room and relaxation area. The treatment suites ensure a guest's total privacy and comfort to fully indulge in the rejuvenation process, while three treatment rooms even have private terraces overlooking the tropical garden pool.

Guests can choose to be pampered with a variety of massage techniques for body and beauty therapies, and Xuan Spa ensures that the combination of relaxing treatments and high-end Italian Comfort Zone products exclusive to Park Hyatt Saigon blend together for an unforgettable spa experience. Refined surroundings and warm welcomes combine to offer a hospitable Vietnamese experience.

ESCAPE FROM REALITY

AQUUM

Kurumba, Maldives

An inner sanctuary of calm and well-being surrounded by a reflection pond of healing water and stunning architecture sets the scene for the care and wisdom that radiates from the AQUUM experience at Kurumba, Maldives.

NAME OF SPA **AQUUM, KURUMBA, MALDIVES**
DESIGN FIRM **C&C DESIGN STUDIO**
IMAGES COURTESY OF **PER AQUUM RESORTS & SPAS**
LOCATION **20-02 NORTH MALE ATOLL, MALDIVES**
TEL **(960) 6642 2324**
WEBSITE **WWW.PERAQUUM.COM**

There are a few places in the world that provide a rejuvenating encounter with nature like AQUUM. The healing spa is set in a pristine location surrounded by water, set in a real and understated environment so that its guests feel relaxed.

AQUUM's architecture draws on the inspiration of Maldives and blends with the wonders of the natural surroundings. Guests feel one with nature as they are guided to their treatment rooms across stones that are surrounded by water. AQUUM reflects healing waters, nature-rich botanicals and indigenous traditions, where each guest is treated as an individual. AQUUM provides a place of calm and quiet, ensuring an escape from reality that is free from distractions.

AQUUM's facilities eight treatment rooms, an aroma steam room, a hydrotherapy pool, refreshing bucket shower, gym, relaxation lounge and yoga pavilion. AQUUM's menu of treatments are created with natural tonics and elixirs made from the life-giving properties of fresh seawater, nutritious sea plants and minerals. From pure waters that cleanse and detoxify to the nutritious ingredients that feed and nourish, the choices are many.

AQUUM's signature treatment includes the Kurumba Spa Escape, where guests can indulge their bodies with a unique foaming exfoliation, using the spa's signature dancing removal technique to soothe skin and leave it silky smooth. This is followed by a symmetry massage finished with a mind ritual designed to de-stress by using a pressure point massage and calming breathing, offering a total escape and an unforgettable spa journey.

COCOA ESCAPE

COMO Shambhala Retreat

Cocoa Island, Maldives

The COMO Shambhala Retreat in Cocoa Island is located in a blissful sanctuary in the Maldives; a beguiling refuge that allows guests to live like a castaway in elegant luxury. It is the island's ultimate point of stillness; tailor-made for those seeking a balance of spiritual and physical renewal.

NAME OF SPA **COMO SHAMBHALA RETREAT, COCOA ISLAND, MALDIVES**
DESIGNER **CHEONG YEW KUAN**
IMAGES COURTESY OF **COMO HOTELS AND RESORTS**
LOCATION **COCOA ISLAND, MAKUNUFUSHI, SOUTH MALE ATOLL, MALDIVES**
TEL **(960) 441 818**
WEBSITE **WWW.COCOAISLAND.COMO.BZ**

The COMO Shambhala Retreat is a place where wellness is nurtured in simple wooden beach houses that are aired by breezes carrying the scent of the ocean. It is housed in contemporary water villas called dhonis, with the architectural accents of traditional Madivian boats and buildings. Decorated in a stylish, elegant and simple way with light and airy rooms, the spa's inspiration is drawn from South Indian and colonial furniture, using local fabrics and traditional colours. Light white cottons with delicate Indian embroidery are seen throughout.

Shambhala translates as "centre of peace and harmony". Guests at the COMO Shambhala Retreat can look forward to a renewal of the body, as well as the rebalancing of the energies. There, they have a complete experience featuring specially-created spa products and treatments, programmes of yoga, meditation and movement exercises, and week-long healing retreats led by world-renowned practitioners.

COMO Shambhala treatments are conducted in the four treatment pavilions (three single and one double), all looking out to sea and with private shower and Jacuzzi gardens. Therapies combine with some of the finest, spiritually-based healing traditions of Asia with natural therapies from the sea and earth, offering a holistic approach to the well-being of the mind and body, for rejuvenation and restored vitality. It is a retreat to withdraw from the world where shady trees strewn with hammocks, quiet corners furnished with day beds and a soothing hydrotherapy pool all offer the space to retire and unwind.

ISLAND GETAWAY

Six Senses Spa

Soneva Fushi, Maldives

Resting on its own private island, Soneva Fushi is the ultimate realisation of the castaway fantasy and a must for weary souls. Located within is the Six Senses Spa, with waterwalls trickling into enclosed pools, giving guests the ultimate in soul therapy.

NAME OF SPA **SIX SENSES SPA, SONEVA FUSHI, MALDIVES**
DESIGN FIRM **SIX SENSES RESORTS & SPAS**
IMAGES COURTESY OF **SIX SENSES RESORTS & SPAS**
LOCATION **KUNFUNADHOO ISLAND, BAA ATOLL, MALDIVES**
TEL **(960) 660 0304**
WEBSITE **WWW.SIXSENSES.COM**

Set privately in a lush jungle and looking towards the surrounding lagoon, the Six Senses Spa at Soneva Fushi offers eleven treatment areas amidst the sight and sound of nature. At the reception, a water pond sets a soothing ambience and a flow of positive energy.

Out of the eleven treatment rooms, five indoor treatment rooms feature water trickling over natural slate walls into indoor rivers, two beach champas offer breathtaking ocean views, two jungle champas offer complete privacy for both day and night usage, and an ayurvedic treatment champa comes with a separate consultation room. A watsu pool is also located near the beach, near the champas. Guest can opt for private Spa Suites at the spa, which are complete with gym facilities.

The spa reflects the resort's charming remoteness, offering the ultimate in barefoot sophistication. Guests experience a luxurious experience in an understated yet sophisticated style, allowing them to enjoy the natural reality of the destination.

With emphasis on holistic therapies, many of the ingredients are grown in the organic vegetable garden before being moulded into nurturing recipes for the face and body. A refreshing range of traditional Maldivian therapies is also available, like the Kurumbaa Kaashi Coconut Rub and the deeply exfoliating Veli Modun Sand Massage, as well as Thai, Balinese, European and doctor-assisted specialised ayurvedic programmes.

One&Only Spa

One&Only Reethi Rah, Maldives

Redefining the concept of the destination spa, One&Only Spa in Reethi Rah is a tranquil island retreat...a place where tension dissolves with the gentle ebb and flow of the Indian Ocean. Here, wellness consultations are on offer for guests seeking holistic, individualised programmes combining fitness, nutrition and beauty treatments.

NAME OF SPA **ONE&ONLY SPA, ONE&ONLY REETHI RAH, MALDIVES**
DESIGN FIRMS **DENNISTON INTERNATIONAL ARCHITECTS AND PLANNERS
AND BENSLEY DESIGN STUDIOS**
IMAGES COURTESY OF **ONE&ONLY RESORTS**
LOCATION **REETHI RAH ISLAND, MALDIVES**
TEL **(960) 6648 800**
WEBSITE **WWW.ONEANDONLYRESORTS.COM**

The One&Only Spa's stylish and haute chic is combined with a diverse Asian influence, blending clean lines with skillful use of natural materials such as coconut shell, sea grass, silk, rattan, teak and thatch. The spa offers a fresh approach to healing traditions in the Maldives. Located on a secluded part of the resort, the spa is brought about by the joint efforts of One& Only Resorts and UK-based spa consultants and operator, ESPA.

With a total spa area of 9,500 square metres, it comprises eight single treatment villas, two double over-water treatment suites, a reception lounge with a lifestyle boutique, hair salon, tai chi pavilions for yoga and relaxation, separate rest areas for men and women, a fitness centre, a world-renowned Bastien Gonzalez Podiatry and Pedicure Clinic, crystal steam rooms and ice fountains.

The ESPA Signature Experiences are a luxurious collection of advanced therapies from around the globe capturing the rituals of the ancient world and combining them with the knowledge and understanding of modern research. Unique skills, a genuine passion for client care and a personal understanding of the needs of each guest are important to ensure each experience is a signature experience.

Guests can choose from the ESPA Energy Equaliser with Volcanic Hot Stones, which uses a powerful combination of pure blended aromatherapy oils, hands-on polarity balancing to regulate electro-magnetic energy and volcanic hot stone massage to release deep-seated tension, or the Reethi Rah Sun Ritual where exfoliating sea salts are combined with nourishing and cooling essential oils to stimulate circulation and soften the skin in preparation for a full body massage with aromatic oils and essential creams.

Taj Spa

Taj Exotica Resort & Spa, Malé

The Taj Spa at the Taj Exotica Resort & Spa in Maldives is the last word in luxury. It is found in an exclusive, private and romantic island resort lush with tropical plants and encircled by clear blue waters of one of the largest lagoons of Maldives.

NAME OF SPA **TAJ SPA, TAJ EXOTICA RESORT & SPA, MALÉ, MAURITIUS**
DESIGN FIRM **JAMES PARK ASSOCIATES**
IMAGES COURTESY OF **TAJ HOTELS, RESORTS AND PALACES**
LOCATION **EMBOODHU FINOLHU, SOUTH MALE ATOLL, MALDIVES**
TEL **(960) 664 2200**
WEBSITE **WWW.TAJHOTELS.COM**

Taj Spa unfolds a refreshing idiom of spa design that emanates a harmonious balance of energy. The sophisticated luxurious and harmonious space incorporates natural elements, resulting in a minimalist yet exotic décor, complemented with elements of Vastushastra – the traditional Indian canon of space planning.

Taj Spa draws inspiration from nature and organic finishes. Fragrant gardens, charming courtyards and panoramic ocean views create an ambience of tranquility and serenity.

Guests can opt for an outdoor massage where views of the calm blue ocean helps lull them into a tranquil state, or an indoor treatment room that also offers the same views.

The spa is the bedrock of wellness. Yoga and meditation as well as ayurveda, aromatherapy and other indigenous Indian therapies as offered by traditional physicians, using exotic Indian ingredients, are the pillars of signature treatments and experiences at Taj Spa.

Guests can take their pick from a variety of Taj Spa treatments and experiences, including the unique two-hour signature experiences such as Sammatva, a treatment that initiates balance of energy centres; Vishuddi, a detoxification treatment; and Vishrama, a deep muscular massage.

INNER SANCTUARY

LIME

Huvafen Fushi, Maldives

A small luxury spa with the world's first underwater massage treatment rooms, LIME is a place where the depth of the water element can be experienced in a sensual treatment. It is where the Indian Ocean merges fluidly with the beauty of the world-class interior spa design.

NAME OF SPA **LIME, HUVAFEN FUSHI, MALDIVES**
DESIGN FIRM **C&C DESIGN STUDIO / RICHARD HYWEL**
IMAGES COURTESY OF **PER AQUUM RESORTS & SPAS**
LOCATION **NORTH MALE ATOLL, MALE, MALDIVES**
TEL **(960) 6644 222**
WEBSITE **WWW.LIMESPAS.COM**

At LIME, guests feel one with nature as their treatments all take place close to the soothing sounds and sights of the Indian Ocean. With six over-water treatment rooms, each with its own glass floor; the world's first underwater spa that offers two double rooms and a separate relaxation area designed specifically for the best vistas of the surrounding sea life; another relaxation area spread over two floors with an aroma-infused steam room, sauna, ice room, high-tech rain shower, boutique, over-water yoga pavilion and gym, it is no wonder LIME has been garnering hype for its design.

The underwater spa at LIME has just undergone an extensive refurbishment by award-winning designer Richard Hywel Evans. The refurbishment features the complete overhaul of the two underwater rooms with a separate relaxation area added. Guests now enter the underwater spa along a passageway lit with colour lighting; think soft pinks, aqua blues, calming yellows and relaxing greens. These colours reflect off the wooden walls on either side of the corridor, which retract to reveal two treatment rooms facing the Indian Ocean and a separate relaxation area straight ahead.

The refurbishment also includes uplifting the interior walls from a light wood to a clean white, allowing greater differentiation of the coloured light, a barisol ceiling and pebble marble tiles under foot, evocative of the sea floor.

A mirror under each massage bed reflects the underwater world of the Maldives, so guests can enjoy the therapeutic touch of the therapist whilst watching the exotic marine life. The Per Aquum Spa Collection has also created two signature massages unique to the underwater spa; with the Unite Me – Crystal Ritual guests can embrace the essence of the Maldives with an indigenous combination of body brushing, sand and lime mineral poultice and coconut oil massage, complete with coconut massage tools designed exclusively by the LIME team at Huvafen Fushi.

GONE FISHING

Taj Spa

Taj Fisherman's Cove, Chennai

Taj Spa from Taj Hotels Resorts and Palaces is the only Indian spa brand in the world with unique Indian signature spa therapies and spa experiences. Offering luxurious Indian wellness signature treatments, their ethos draws on the rich and ancient wellness heritage of India; the fabled lifestyle and culture of Indian royalty through the centuries; and the healing therapies that embrace Indian spirituality.

NAME OF SPA TAJ SPA, TAJ FISHERMAN'S COVE, CHENNAI, INDIA
DESIGN FIRM TAJ HOTELS, RESORTS AND PALACES
IMAGES COURTESY OF TAJ HOTELS, RESORTS AND PALACES
LOCATION COVELONG BEACH, KANCHIPURAM DISTRICT 603 112, TAMIL NADU, INDIA
TEL (91) 44 6741 3333
WEBSITE WWW.TAJHOTELS.COM

Taj Spa at Taj Fisherman's Cove is located in arguably the best luxury five-star resort in South India. Located on a stretch of powder-white beach, set amongst 22 acres of gracefully swaying towering casuarinas and palm trees, Fisherman's Cove with its spectacular view of the deep blue yonder, is a heavenly place to unwind.

It is at this slice of paradise that Taj Spa is found, bringing together the wisdom and heritage of the Asian and Indian philosophy of wellness and well-being, guiding guests towards a life of physical, mental and spiritual equilibrium. Rooted in ancient Indian healing knowledge, Taj Spa derives inspiration and spirit from the holistic concept of living. Yoga; Meditation, mastered and disseminated by accomplished practitioners; Ayurveda and indigenous traditional Indian body therapies form the pillars of the Taj experience.

Designed in a minimalist style with touches that reflect the elements of nature, the Taj Spa is equipped with single treatment rooms, double treatment suites, meditation and yoga pavilion with a separate ayurveda enclave with thatched huts, swimming pool and a fully-equipped gym and a beauty salon amongst others. Signature Taj Spa experience facilities bring in secret rejuvenation and engaging experiences from the splendor of Regal India.

Blending ancient Indian wisdom with contemporary therapies, the Taj Spa unveils the best in Indian rejuvenation therapies ranging from Indian aromatherapy massages, time-honored Indian treatments, body scrubs and wraps. Contributing their skill to the wellness experience are trained practitioners of ayurveda, meditation, yoga as well as Indian and other signature body therapies.

EVERGREEN PRESENCE

Taj Spa

Taj Green Cove Resort, Kovalam

A unique combination of a beach resort, backwater escape, hill retreat and spa, the Taj Green Cove Resort, Kovalam, invites guests to savour the true essence of the scenic coastal state of Kerala.

NAME OF SPA **TAJ SPA, TAJ GREEN COVE RESORT, KOVALAM, INDIA**
DESIGN FIRM **RDM DESIGN**
IMAGES COURTESY OF **TAJ HOTELS, RESORTS AND PALACES**
LOCATION **G.V. RAJA VATTAPARA ROAD, KOVALAM, TRIVANDRUM, KERALA, INDIA**
TEL **(91) 471 248 7733**
WEBSITE **WWW.TAJHOTELS.COM**

With detailing in pristine white and earthy wood finishes that tender a soothing, calm ambience, Taj Spa at the resort is breathtaking. Unwind and take in the view at the relaxation lounge as it overlooks a private waterfall garden courtyard. This tropical style landscape is a magical mix of local ethos and heritage in a contemporary setting. It resides a refreshing mix of style and spacious elegance, offering guests a soothing ambience overlooking beautifully landscaped gardens.

Equipped with single and double treatment suites that are bordered by garden courtyards and water features, the Taj Spa offers treatments and programmes specially designed to maintain physical, mental and spiritual equilibrium. Enjoy yoga in the yoga lounge or on the golden sands of the beach. The spa's communal wet area encompasses a steam bath and an open-air Jacuzzi with a panoramic view of the ocean.

Blending ancient Indian wisdom with contemporary therapies, Taj Spa unveils the best in Indian rejuvenation therapies ranging from Indian aromatherapy massages, time-honoured Indian treatments, body scrubs and wraps, yoga & meditation. A well-equipped gymnasium, a beauty room and spa shop are some of the other indulgences here.

This idyllic spa setting is just what the doctor ordered for wearisome souls looking for that perfect moment of bliss and serenity.

URBAN RETREAT

Quan Spa

JW Marriott Mumbai, India

Quan Mumbai is the first urban spa retreat for the spa group. Complementing resort spas in Sanya, Koh Samui and the soon-to-be-opened flagship spa in Bali, the 297-square-metre tranquility zone is a haven where guests are encouraged to leave the decision-making at the door.

NAME OF SPA **QUAN SPA, JW MARRIOTT MUMBAI, INDIA**
DESIGNER **ZORAN DZUNIC**
IMAGES COURTESY OF **JW MARRIOTT**
LOCATION **JUHU TARA ROAD, JUHU BEACH, MUMBAI 400049, INDIA**
TEL **(91) 22 6693 3000**
WEBSITE **WWW.MARRIOTT.COM**

Designed in collaboration with Zoran Dzunic, the spa successfully integrates design with operational use. The adage "form follows function" can be seen in all areas of the spa, from the reception and waiting areas right through to the treatment rooms. Here, subtle influences of India's religious and cultural heritage are combined with a modern, cutting-edge design.

The spa comprises eight spacious private treatment suites, a Vichy shower room and a couple's treatment room. Behind translucent perspex doors that allow form but not detail to be seen, treatment rooms contain private shower and changing facilities. Room fit-out is kept to a minimum, relying on the use of colour and light to provide a calming effect on guests.

Representing calm, the warm orange colour of the corridor, treatment rooms with soft neutral-coloured walls, bamboo flooring, warm natural woods within the changing facilities and natural stone and pebbles in oversized showers add to an ambience that soothes. Keeping Mumbai's chaotic streets in mind, the first design thought was to create a space where guests can instantly seek refuge in a white, pristine and clean place.

In a spa where rooms are individualised by use of accent colours borrowed from the Indian system of Chakras, the ceiling coffers above the massage beds are used as a wall surface with various water of feather images placed to further give a sense of lightness while guests are having a treatment. Handpicked artefacts from Kerala, the centre of India's rediscovered traditional ayurveda therapies, are sprinkled throughout the spa, giving the space an unmistakable Indian character.

A range of spa packages based on the five elements of fire, water, air, earth and space are offered here. These treatments are tailored to enhance their balancing properties for the appropriate dosha (or body type) and include a mix of traditional treatments, ayurvedic treatments and lifestyle therapies such as yoga.

DESIGNER HAVEN

Bulgari Spa

Bulgari Resort Bali, Indonesia

Designed by the famed Antonio Citterio, the Bulgari Spa offers the ultimate luxurious resort spa experience where traditional Balinese culture and the elegance of Italian contemporary style are reflected in the exquisite design.

NAME OF SPA **BULGARI SPA, BULGARI RESORT BALI, INDONESIA**
DESIGN FIRM **ANTONIO CITTERIO & PARTNERS**
IMAGES COURTESY OF **BVLGARI HOTELS AND RESORTS**
LOCATION **JALAN GOA LEMPEH, BANJAR DINAS KANGIN, ULUWATU, BALI 80364, INDONESIA**
TEL **(62) 361 847 1000**
WEBSITE **WWW.BULGARIHOTELS.COM**

Bulgari Spa is dramatically and romantically located on a high cliff top with breathtaking views overlooking the Indian Ocean. A complete retreat from the rest of the world, the spa extends an enticing invitation for guests to enter a seductive world of peace and harmony. Italian masters of geometry, Antonio Citterio & Partners, known for their style and colour, incorporated indigenous materials, expressing themselves with the traditional hand-cut volcanic stones and rich exotic woods. Expect refined contemporary design, Italian in birthright, accentuated sensitively to respect its Balinese context.

In addition to the beautiful spa treatment villas, pure indulgence can be experienced by reserving one of the exclusive private Spa Pavilions offering spacious and luxurious facilities for personal or shared escapism. Each couple's pavilion contains a whirlpool bath and outdoor living space with an open air shower. The Royal Private Spa Pavilion benefits from the addition of a luxurious Steam Shower and secluded, outdoor Plunge Pool.

The Private Spa Pavilions are a haven of exclusive tranquility for a minimum of three or more hours, and includes relaxation time before and after treatments, encouraging guests to enjoy the stunning surroundings of their pavilion.

Internationally-acclaimed ESPA has created a range of sophisticated therapies of Balinese, Asian and European origins, all enriched by attentive and graceful Balinese service. Guests experience a ritualistic journey to find balance, peace and tranquility as the spa's team of professional, ESPA-trained therapists creates a customised sequence of therapies to suit their personal needs.

Banyan Tree Spa

Bintan, Indonesia

Banyan Tree Bintan was the first resort to open on the island and is without a doubt one of the island's most exclusive. Located in the Riau archipelago on the private beach of Tanjong Said, this spa features 64 villas built into the forested slopes above a bay.

NAME OF SPA **BANYAN TREE SPA BINTAN, INDONESIA**
DESIGN FIRM **ARCHITRAVE DESIGN AND PLANNING**
IMAGES COURTESY OF **BANYAN TREE**
LOCATION **JALAN TELUK BEREMBANG, LAGUNA BINTAN, LAGOI 29155, BINTAN RESORTS, INDONESIA**
TEL **(62) 7706 93100**
WEBSITE **WWW.BANYANTREESPA.COM/BINTAN**

Within a rustic Asian environment, guests are at liberty to appreciate the wonders of nature that surrounds the spa as this award-winning resort is built on alleviated surroundings that offer breathtaking views of the South China Sea. Villas modelled after traditional Balinese architecture are designed and decorated with a colloquial flavour.

Each villa is raised on stilts, perched on hillsides with stunning views of the bay below, offering guests a unique tree-top experience. Guest are also given the choice of villas overlooking the South China Sea, Tanjong Said Bay or the lush tropical valley. An added bonus is definitely the 18-hole championship golf course designed by Greg Norman.

A sanctuary for the senses, Banyan Tree Spa Bintan is designed as a realm of pampering and guests can select from a range of treatment therapies from the exotic and traditional royal Javanese Lulur and Balinese Boreh to the more modern European rejuvenation therapies such hydrotherapy and massotherapy.

One can also opt for the signature Royal Banyan and Rainmist treatment packages for an indulgent experience. The fresh ingredients used during treatments are prepared on a daily basis and the spa's hospitable therapists are trained at the Banyan Tree Spa Academy in Phuket.

Mandara Spa

Nikko Bali Resort & Spa, Indoneisa

Mandara Spa in Nikko Bali Resort & Spa is tucked neatly into the resort's lush tropical gardens. Complemented by eight open-air Spa Villas by the beach, the spa is nestled away in a resort that features a spectacular panoramic view of the Indian Ocean.

NAME OF SPA **MANDARA SPA, NIKKO BALI RESORT & SPA, INDONESIA**
DESIGNER **MR I GEDE KUSUMAWIJAYA**
IMAGES COURTESY OF **MANDARA SPA**
LOCATION **JALAN RAYA NUSA DUA SELATAN, NUSA DUA 80363, INDONESIA**
TEL **(62) 3617 73377**
WEBSITE **WWW.MANDARASPA.COM**

Mandara Spa offers a range of spa experiences, instilled with the beauty and allure of Balinese traditions in the hushed havens of traditional style villas, successfully emulating a traditional Balinese village.

Open-air villas represent the houses while surrounding lush vegetation and fragrant tropical flowers bring a sense of rustic village life. This combination provides the ideal ambience for relaxation and rejuvenation.

The Mandara Spa winds its way up from the beach and settles sublimely into the tropical vegetation at the edge of the resort. The complex comprises the spa reception, boutique, four indoor treatment suites and two open air treatment rooms, in addition to the eight deluxe double spa villas.

These traditional, open-air villas are designed for peaceful pampering, escape and tranquil indulgence. Set behind high stone walls, they each feature a covered and fan-cooled treatment area for two people, outdoor showers, lush tropical foliage, water fountains and a large, shaded outdoor Jacuzzi.

The treatment range at Mandara Spa includes massages, facials, body scrubs, spa manicure and pedicure, and indulgent spa combination packages.

Soothing Spirituality

COMO Shambhala Retreat

Uma Ubud, Bali

The COMO Shambhala Retreat located in Uma Ubud overlooks the Tjampuhan Valley amid paddy fields carved out of hillsides, backed by coconut palms and banyan trees.

NAME OF SPA **COMO SHAMBHALA RETREAT, UMA UBUD, BALI**
DESIGNER **KOICHIRO IKEBUCHI**
PHOTOGRAPHY BY **KELLEY CHENG**
LOCATION **JALAN RAYA SANGGINGAN, BANJAR LUNGSIAKAN, KEDEWATAN, UBUD, GIANYAR 80571, BALI, INDONESIA**
TEL **(62) 3619 72448**
WEBSITE **HTTP://UMA.COMO.BZ**

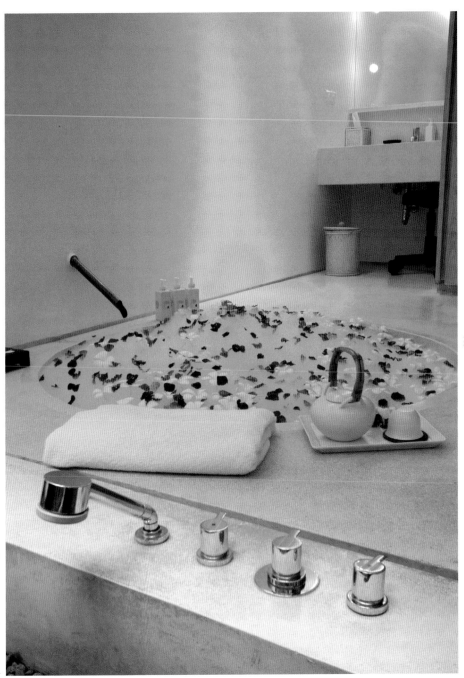

The COMO Shambhala Retreat is located in a three-hectare hotel site hidden on the fringe of Ubud, with the river Oos running below and the mountain on one side. There is no sound of traffic. The town, where there are numerous shops, galleries and local restaurants, is a five-minute drive, or 20-minute walk. The retreat is open, clean and landscaped simply. Japanese designer Koichiro Ikebuchi is responsible for the retreat's interior aesthetic, designed to feel like a rural home in the hills. Indigenous materials include local woods and alang-alang thatched roofs.

The COMO Shambhala Retreat was developed in recognition of Bali's powerful spirituality. It was designed for guests seeking greater health through yoga and related treatments. The open-air pavilion for group and private yoga practice has the best views in all the resort. In addition, find a meditation bale, a reflexology area, steam, sauna, gym, four treatment rooms and a 25-metre jade green pool.

The Asian-based therapies range from specific body treatments to facials to sophisticated massages, including the COMO Shambhala signature massages, delivered by experienced practitioners who customise treatments according to individual needs. Guests may also want to try The Uma Bath, a cleansing treatment that works gently to exfoliate and soften skin. After dry brushing the body, COMO Shambhala's specially-prepared Invigorate Salt Scrub (infused with essential oils, macadamia oil and oat bran) is applied to the body. This is followed by a revitalising bath and concludes with a relaxing COMO Shambhala massage.

SERENE ESTATE

COMO Shambhala Estate

Begawan Giri, Bali

COMO Shambhala Estate, which is a unique residential health retreat located in Bali, is found in an inland jungle on a peaceful riverbank. It is a place where spring water is sacred, revered by Balinese for its healing properties.

NAME OF SPA **COMO SHAMBHALA ESTATE, BEGAWAN GIRI, BALI**
DESIGNER **KOICHIRO IKEBUCHI**
PHOTOGRAPHY BY **KELLEY CHENG**
LOCATION **BANJAR BEGAWAN, MELINGGIH KELOD, BALI, INDONESIA**
TEL **(62) 3619 78888**
WEBSITE **HTTP://CSE.COMOSHAMBHALA.BZ**

Just as in the oldest spa traditions, The Estate's location is predicated upon the existence of The Source, a natural spring on site that has long been revered by locals for its healing properties. The Balinese have always used this spring in conjunction with the profusion of unique medicinal plants that grow in the surrounding forest.

Water from The Source fills Kedara, which is Sanskrit for "Water Garden". This is a unique area of The Estate, located at one remove from the main property down numerous stone steps. Guests pass through the forest, towards the edge of the River Ayung. There are four treatment bales, relaxation areas and small, fresh pools. There is also a hot tub, and perched a little higher, The Estate's Pilates Studio. The spirit is unique. The only sounds are of the forest's birdlife and the gentle flow of water as it runs close by. Many guests wander down to simply read a book, to meditate or catch up on much-needed sleep. Others come for specific treatments, as per their condition, with recommendations made by The Estate's resident naturopath.

Further exploiting the power of water is The Estate's Vitality Pool. This is found at Ojas (Sanskrit for "Essence of Life"), which is the main treatment area located at the property's heart. The water is chlorine-free and using a bio energy water treatment system, is kept soft and clear. It can help heal skin rashes. It is also anti-ageing. High pressure jets are employed for massage and also for exercise.

Likewise, the accommodation at the Estate is unique, consisting of large villas built in the forest. These include Tirta-Ening ("Clear Water"), a residence dominated by a 91-square-metre principal suite with an exquisite Japanese water garden featuring a private waterfall. The entire residence has a Zen feel. The sound of water can be heard throughout. Also of note are the new Retreat Villas, Taramala ("Garland of Stars") and Vasudhara ("Mother Earth"). Both feature private therapy rooms and personal pools – again, harnessing water to help create the perfect healing environment.

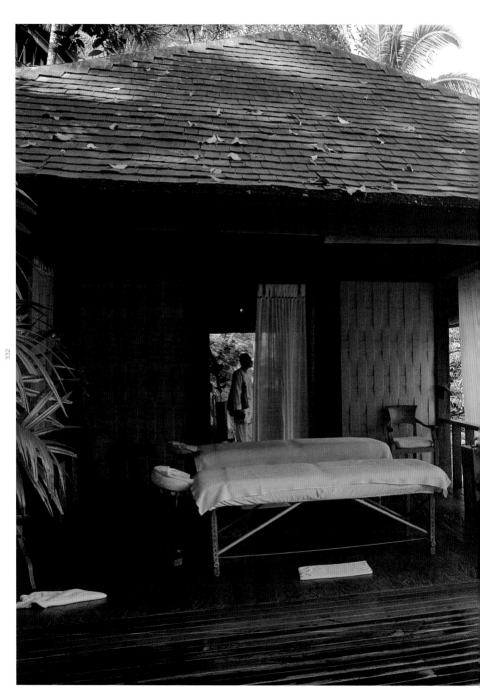

KEEPING WITH TRADITION

The Spa at The Legian

Bali, Indonesia

Set in the idyllic grounds of landscaped tropical gardens, The Spa at The Legian offers treatments in luxurious surroundings that never lose sight of their traditional roots.

NAME OF SPA **THE SPA AT THE LEGIAN, BALI, INDONESIA**
DESIGNERS **GRAHACIPTA HADIPRANA AND JAYA IBRAHIM**
PHOTOGRAPHY BY **KELLEY CHENG**
LOCATION **JALAN LAKSMANA, SEMINYAK BEACH, BALI 80361**
TEL **(62) 3617 30622**
WEBSITE **WWW.GHMHOTELS.COM**

As The Spa at The Legian is located by the ocean, the focus of the entire property is the sea – the relentless sound of waves from the Indian Ocean rolling in on the secluded stretch of beach. The interior designer used the ocean as inspiration throughout the spa's décor.

The spa is located in a four-storey building that makes reference to Balinese temple and palace architecture but with a decidedly modern spin. On top of the building are structures that hark back to the Balinese Kulkul towers (Bale Kulkul), from which villagers are called to the temple by the beating of the wooden signal drum. The spa features smooth marble floors and intricate Indonesian sculptures, taking Balinese traditions of design and form and presenting them in a contemporary manner.

The spa consists of two double and two single Spa Suites, which feature views of the Indian Ocean. Surrounded by lotus ponds and stone walkways, the suites create an area of serenity and relaxation. A fully-equipped gym, steam room, manicure and pedicure lounge, and additional double suite are located in a separate garden area offering an extensive range of massage, beauty and health treatments.

The Spa at The Legian's relaxing range of signature treatments includes the Wave Massage where guests are nurtured with long massage movements, very much like waves caressing their bodies; and The Legian Massage, which is a dynamic fusion of five massage styles including Shiatsu, Thai, Swedish, Balinese and Hawaiian Lomi Lomi, with two therapists working in synchronisation to lull guests into a blissful state.

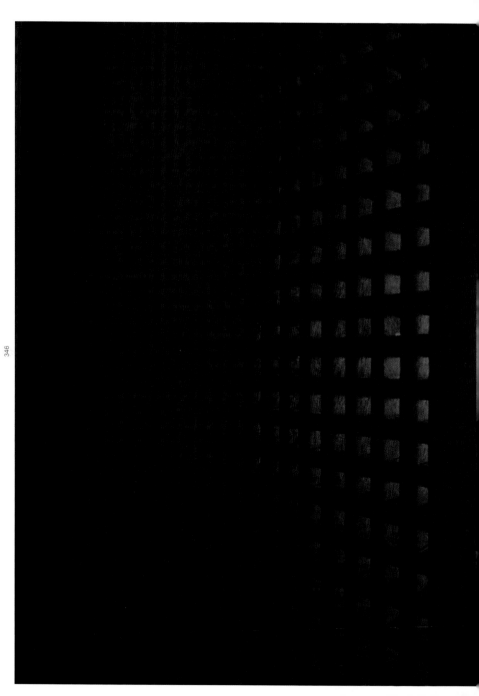

CHI, the Spa

Shangri-La's Rasa Sayang Resort & Spa

The concept of CHI is to create a sanctuary of tranquillity inspired by the legend of "Shangri-La." One of the main hallmarks of CHI is spacious, private spa suites and villas, designed to create a "spa within a spa" environment. Therapies are based on the ancient healing traditions, philosophies and rituals of China and the Himalayas.

NAME OF SPA CHI, THE SPA AT SHANGRI-LA'S RASA SAYANG RESORT & SPA, MALAYSIA
DESIGN FIRM DESIGN BJ.BE
IMAGES COURTESY OF SHANGRI-LA'S RASA SAYANG RESORT & SPA
LOCATION BATU FERINGGI 11100, PENANG, MALAYSIA
TEL (60) 4888 8888
WEBSITE WWW.SHANGRI-LA.COM

This concept is further enhanced at CHI, the Spa at Shangri-La's Rasa Sayang Resort & Spa by local cultural influences in architecture and interior design, treatment techniques and ingredients, and the luxuriant tropical landscape that has always been synonymous with Rasa Sayang Resort.

This first CHI Spa in Malaysia will be a veritable sanctuary within 3,800 square metres of gardens complete with eleven treatment villas, yoga studio, reception and sanctum, all set amidst lush gardens beside one of the hotel's private pools. Of the treatment villas, there will be three Couples' Villas and eight Garden Suites – some with outdoor spa tubs and designed in keeping with CHI's signature "spa within a spa" concept with private changing, vanity, relaxation and bathroom facilities.

The spa area is enveloped by walls made of local granite, shaded by the canopy of century-old rain trees and intersected by walkways through bamboo forests. All spa structures are open to the surrounding tropical vegetation. Tranquil interiors include teak walls, wood tiles and rich, dark silks, highlighted by Chinese, Himalayan and Malaysian art and artefacts.

Treatments at CHI, the Spa at Shangri-La's Rasa Sayang Resort & Spa are also distinguished by their Peranakan aspect. Peranakan culture is a result of Portuguese, Dutch, British, Malay and Indonesian influences on the old immigrant Chinese community that settled in Malacca, Penang and Singapore.

Exotic local ingredients appear throughout CHI's menu of more than 25 treatments – from poultices of lemon grass and ginger to oil of nutmeg and aromatic pandan leaves used in body treatments. The Rasa Asmaradana massage treatment and Rasa Nyaman body wrap, each involving traditional Malaysian techniques and ingredients, are destined to become signature therapies, opening a window to local Malay ritual and healing culture to contemporary spa-goers.

TROPICAL DESTINATION

Mandara Spa

Sunway Resort Hotel & Spa, Malaysia

The Mandara Spa at Sunway Resort Hotel & Spa embodies the essence of an Asian-inspired spa with tranquility, therapy and relaxation packaged in a luscious tropical setting of 4,200 square metres.

NAME OF SPA **MANDARA SPA, SUNWAY RESORT HOTEL & SPA, MALAYSIA**
DESIGN FIRM **TID DESIGN (M) SDN BHD**
IMAGES COURTESY OF **MANDARA SPA**
LOCATION **PERSIARAN LAGOON, BANDAR SUNWAY, 46150, PETALING JAYA, SELANGOR DARUL EHSAN, MALAYSIA**
TEL **(60) 3 7495 2080**
WEBSITE **WWW.MANDARASPA.COM**

The spa's assault on the senses lies in strolling through the verdant greenery where an indulgent feeling sets in even before you commence your spa experience. Guests are taken on a journey through its lush gardens and just beyond its golden hardwood main entrance doorframe is a Moorish-like structure that houses a novel Manicure & Pedicure Pavillion.

Past the first cluster of treatment suites and into the oversized reception area cum spa boutique, it becomes evident that the Mandara Spa with its intense use of wood, water, soft yellow lights and pastel colours reflects a puzzle of earth tones. Constructed with high quality local materials, the property combines the best of Balinese architectural elements with contemporary flair and elegant finishes. Open spaces infused with rays of natural sunlight are coupled with ceiling-high glass windows on the opposite side to present a blend of outdoor living and air-conditioned comfort, simultaneously bringing in the inspirational outdoors into the interior for a sense of seamlessness.

Mandara Spa, which sits on the highest peak of the resort, adopts a contemporary ambience with hints of Balinese culture, showcases ten spacious, private Spa Suites. Treatment suites are designed for singles and couples alike. There are two Double Deluxe Spa Suites with their own en suite steam-shower room, three Single Spa Suites with en suite steam-shower room, three Single Spa Suites and two Royal Thai Massage treatment suites.

Upon completion of a treatment, guests are encouraged to prolong the sensorial journey by stepping onto the overhanging timber verandah flanked by lotus ponds and fringed by a forest of trees. The daybed is an ideal place to absorb not just the surrounding nature, but also to listen to the ceaseless gurgle of the cascading water from the waterfall below. The Mandara Spa at Sunway Resort Hotel & Spa is undeniably a sensorial haven just minutes from the city.

BACK TO NATURE

The Spa

The Andaman, Langkawi

Given its magnificent location nestled between the Datai Bay and a virgin tropical rainforest on the Malaysian island of Langkawi, The Spa at Andaman's architects Jalex Sdn Bhd and Dato' Zainal Abidin didn't have to think long before deciding to incorporate nature's offerings into the design.

NAME OF SPA **THE SPA, THE ANDAMAN, LANGKAWI, MALAYSIA**
DESIGN FIRM **DATO' ZAINAL ABIDIN – DBA AKITEK / JALEX SDN BHD**
IMAGES COURTESY OF **THE ANDAMAN**
LOCATION **JALAN TELUK DATAI, 07000 PALAU LANGKAWI, KEDAH DARUL AMAN, MALAYSIA**
TEL **(60) 4959 1088**
WEBSITE **WWW.THEANDAMAN.COM**

The Spa pays homage to tradition with its thatched roofs and airy rooms painted in shades of white and offering highlights in wood. The steeped roofing is supported by great wooden poles so popular in the region, turning spa treatments into an open-air affair. The uniquely designed spa, featuring spectacular panoramic views, is set into the hillside adjacent to the resort overlooking beautiful Datai Bay. The rejuvenating influence of the vast Andaman Sea, the healing essence of the rainforest and the delights of natural spices, flowers and pure fresh air blend to create traditional body treatments for the pleasure of its guests.

Rainforest Villas are duplex-style overlooking the blue Andaman Seas and include two massage beds on each level, large bathtub, garden shower and relaxation terrace. The Sari Villa, a very private villa, offers more lavish facilities including a large Jacuzzi, relaxation balai and garden-shower.

At The Spa, guests can choose from a range of signature treatments including the Traditional Thai Massage, which is a two-hour session employing an ancient technique that stretches and uses pressure point work to balance the flow of qi through energy channels known as sen lines; the Wave Massage, where long fluid movements flow rhythmically like waves caressing the body; and the Organic Facial, which is a six-step facial with pure products based on organic herbal ingredients.

The Oriental Spa

The Oriental, Singapore

Located on the fifth level of The Oriental, Singapore, the 528-square-metre spa comprises four luxurious treatment rooms, a couple's suite, a Shiatsu room, a private Relaxation Lounge and a high-performance exercise studio.

NAME OF SPA **THE ORIENTAL SPA, THE ORIENTAL, SINGAPORE**
DESIGN FIRM **COOMBS ASSOCIATES**
IMAGES COURTESY OF **THE ORIENTAL, SINGAPORE**
LOCATION **5 RAFFLES AVENUE, MARINA SQUARE, SINGAPORE 039797**
TEL **(65) 6338 0066**
WEBSITE **WWW.MANDARINORIENTAL.COM**

The innovative and restorative treatments at The Oriental Spa merge both ancient and modern techniques and philosophies from around the world, using 100 per cent pure essential oils and herbs. The Oriental Spa aspires to provide each guest with a personalised sensory journey to wellness, focusing on the six senses.

In keeping with its sense of place and reinforcing the exotic roots of Mandarin Oriental, the spa is both contemporary and reflective of the surrounding Asian cultures. Tranquility and harmony are the inspiration behind the design of the spa; features include walnut timber flooring and Asian motif panels, complemented with traditional Chinese furniture.

Each guest embarks on his or her journey of the senses upon entering the spa. A Relaxation Lounge has been specially designed for guests to unwind and relax before and after treatments, where they can individually listen to calming music. Each treatment begins with a soothing foot ritual while the spa therapist assesses the guest's individual needs.

Couples or friends who wish to share their spa experience may choose to have their treatments in the spacious 62-square-metre couple's suite. Equipped with two beautiful Agape baths and a steam room, guests can begin their spa experience with a fresh flower bath and an invigorating steam bath. A separate relaxation area offers a comforting opium bed, provides a perfect haven for guests to float back to reality at their own leisurely pace after the treatment ends.

The Oriental Spa's signature treatments include The Oriental Massage, a unique treatment that combines the best of all forms of Asian massage to create a soothing and pampering experience. The Oriental Spa uses Aromatherapy Associates products for its treatments. The pure essential oils used will depend on each guest's requirements, which will be determined during consultation before each treatment.

RAFFLES OASIS

RafflesAmrita Spa

Raffles The Plaza, Singapore

The flagship of Amrita spas worldwide, RafflesAmrita Spa is an oasis of paradise spread over 50,000 square feet where guests can escape the pressures of a busy day and rediscover a quality lifestyle within a convenient urban setting.

NAME OF SPA **RAFFLESAMRITA SPA, RAFFLES THE PLAZA, SINGAPORE**
DESIGN FIRM **RICHMOND INTERNATIONAL**
IMAGES COURTESY OF **RAFFLES THE PLAZA, SINGAPORE**
LOCATION **80 BRAS BASAH ROAD, LEVEL 6, SINGAPORE 189560**
TEL **(65) 6336 4477**
WEBSITE **WWW.AMRITASPAS.COM**

In Sanskit, "Amrita" refers to the magical elixir of eternal youth and this peaceful retreat aims to cater to a guest's total well-being and renewal. With over 35 treatment rooms and VIP suites including a private Jacuzzi, aroma steam bath and private showers, guests are pampered with an integrated range of spa and skin care services, fitness facilities, the brand's own private label of aromatherapy products and nutritious spa cuisine for the health-conscious. Although the male and female treatment areas segregated for greater comfort and privacy, couples can opt to undergo treatments together by utilising the VIP suites.

At RafflesAmrita Spa, the clean simple lines create an understated and tranquil environment designed to appeal to the senses. An interplay of soothing (earth-tone) and vibrant (yellow, green and blue) colours, together with signature lighting features, complete the unique design, look and feel of the spa. Right from the moment guests enter the spa, they are greeted by the sound of gently cascading water at the entrance. The interchange of soothing colours and furnishings around the spa make for a truly idyllic sojourn. In each softly-lit treatment room that is gently fragranced, relaxing piped-in music puts the guest in a state of relaxation – a befitting start to the spa experience.

Home to one of the largest spa facilities in Asia, the spa features an extensive menu of treatments that was created from combining the best of Eastern and Western philosophies and methodologies. One of their signature treatments includes the popular skin rejuvenator, the Anti-Aging Caviar Facial. Rich in nutrients, the decadent facial is the crème de la crème of spa treatments. Guests can also choose form a choice of water therapies that aid in overall health and wellness, such as Aroma / Herbal Hydro Fusion, Hydro Massage and Tropical Rain Shower. With great service and exotic treatments, it is no wonder the spa has won a host of accolades, including the coveted Best Hotel Spa for the second consecutive year at the SpaAsia Crystal Awards 2005.

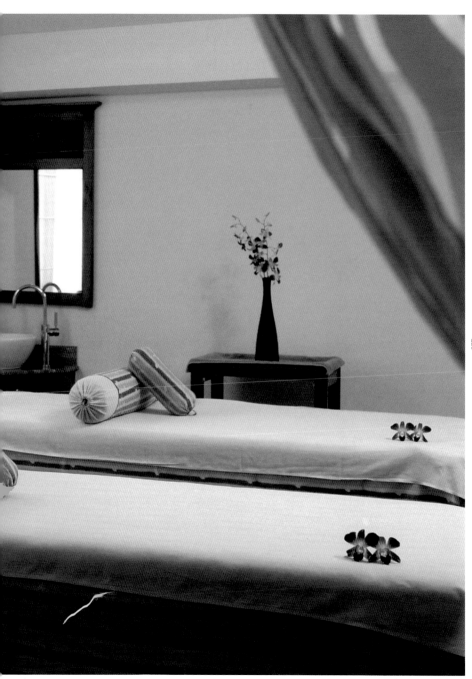

Treat

Red White & Pure, Singapore

Located in what is believed to be the first holistic and lifestyle store at Red White & Pure is Treat, a spa where extensive knowledge and heritage is brought to life in this authentic Traditional Chinese Medicine (TCM) wellness retreat that aims to banish your stress away.

NAME OF SPA **TREAT, RED WHITE & PURE, SINGAPORE**
DESIGN FIRM **IN-HOUSE DESIGN TEAM, RED WHITE & PURE**
IMAGES COURTESY OF **RED WHITE & PURE**
LOCATION **1 HARBOURFRONT WALK, #02-141 VIVOCITY, SINGAPORE 098585**
TEL **(65) 6827 0088**
WEBSITE **WWW.REDWHITEPURE.COM**

Guests leave their worries behind when they step into the calm and serene space that is Treat. Six cocoon-shaped rooms (including a luxurious coupl's room) provide the calm location for guests to unwind and relax. Inspired by nature, the cocoons can be conceived as a sign of metamorphosis, akin to a butterfly's cocoon where guests enter for a relaxing treat and leave rejuvenated. It is also reminiscent of a mother's womb, where guests are comforted with feelings of security.

The white cocoons are complemented with brown walls, accented with splashes of red in the form of furniture pieces. Found alongside the cocoons is Touch, a sanctuary where guests come together to meditate and heal. At the reception, giant lily pads adorn the floor space, each housing a myriad of products designed to enhance the guest's holistic journey.

At Treat, only quality natural ingredients and techniques from Zing, Aromatherapy Associates and Dr Hauschka are used. Signature treatments include the Aroma Treat, which is a true aromatherapy massage combining pure essential oils with a specialised massage for the body; or the Orient Ex-stress, which is a deep and meaningful all-over body massage that is a serious treatment to banish one's stress. The service here is topnotch, and your host-cum-therapist ensures that you entire stay is a holistic and pleasant one, ensuring that you leave Treat truly de-stressed.

SECLUDED SANCTUARY

CHI, The Spa

Shangri-La's Mactan Island Resort & Spa

The CHI, the Spa at Shangri-La's Mactan Island Resort & Spa is reminiscent of a secluded sanctuary inspired by the legend of "Shangri-La" captured in James Hilton's tome *Lost Horizon*.

NAME OF SPA **CHI, THE SPA AT SHANGRI-LA'S MACTAN ISLAND RESORT & SPA**, CEBU, PHILIPPINES
DESIGN FIRM **DESIGN B.U. BE**
IMAGES COURTESY OF **SHANGRI-LA's MACTAN ISLAND RESORT & SPA**
LOCATION **PUNTA ENGANO ROAD, LAPU-LAPU CITY 6015, PHILIPPINES**
TEL **(63) 32 2310 288**
WEBSITE **WWW.SHANGRI-LA.COM/SPA**

Covering a vast area of over 10,000 square metres, CHI, the Spa at Shangri-La's Mactan Island Resort & Spa is one of the largest spa resorts in the Philippines. With extensive spa gardens and treatment pavilions, six villas measuring 135 square metres complete with private patios, sunken bathing tubs and relaxing lounges, and eight garden suites, CHI provides the luxury of personal space and timelessness.

The CHI experience commences at the entrance, fronted by a large sculptural brick fountain and water cascade representing the five elements of metal, water, wood, fire and earth. At the Sanctum, a three-tiered open air sanctuary houses the reception, boutique and lounge, while an intricate glass sculpture suspended from the ceiling adds to the aesthetics of the milieu. From its calm serenity, guests can enjoy the CHI Water Garden Pavilion that features an infinity edge vitality pool and body scrub salas before selecting from a menu of over 30 face and body treatments, massages and water therapies. Developed by a team of experts in traditional Chinese medicine and Himalayan healing traditions, the CHI Spa Village's signature therapies are based on the five elements theory, in which all the elements are in balance to harmonise with the positive yang and negative yin energy within the body.

Drawing inspiration from a myriad of sources, the CHI design team added touches from the gardens of China's highlands to the halls of the Patan Museum in Kathmandu. Working with local artisans in the Himalayas, the intricate wood detailing found throughout the building structures reflects traditional Tibetan and Nepelase architectural features, while the bronze lotus flower inlays found throughout the pathways were made in Nepal through the traditional "lost wax" process. Wooden frames highlighting Himalayn artefacts are suspended as if in mid-air from interlocking hand-wrought metal straps

As it is based in the Philippines, CHI, the Spa at Shangri-La's Mactan Island Resort & Spa also uses elements from the country. The buildings' facings are constructed from Mactan stone that is hewn from coral deposits found throughout the island, while the interior furnishings are handcrafted by local Cebuano artists.

DIVINE VIEWS

Q1 Spa

Queensland, Australia

Here at Q1 Spa, good things come in twos: this award-winning spa specialises in treatments for couples, best friends, and mothers and daughters. Though spread over two levels, Q1 Spa's unusual design evokes the feeling of a single level disappearing into the surrounding lagoon at first glance, set in the luxurious gardens of the world's tallest residential building.

NAME OF SPA **Q1 SPA**
DESIGN FIRM **DBI DESIGN**
IMAGES COURTESY OF **EXCLUSIVE SPAS GROUP AUSTRALIA**
LOCATION **HAMILTON AVENUE, SURFERS PARADISE, QUEENSLAND 4127, AUSTRALIA**
TEL **(61) 7 5539 9293**
WEBSITE **WWW.ESPA.NET.AU**

Q1 Spa sits like a mirage – floating in an enormous lagoon pool amidst the gardens of the iconic Q1 Resort, the design of the spa creates an exquisite sanctuary within Australia's most bustling tourist destination – Surfer's Paradise. Combining therapeutic and holistic wellness with a touch of spirituality, all treatments here begin with a traditional rite of passage.

The treatment rooms and reception area at Q1 Spa are larger by usual standards to ensure a sense of openness. A glass enclosed external hot tub was incorporated to allow the walkways and open areas on the lower level to be bathed in natural light. Boasting eight ambient treatment rooms, both wet and dry, the rooms are minimalist in style, with cabinetry in whipped honey coloured granite. Clean lines and functional design create an ambience of elegance and warmth. Large river stones strategically placed through out the building complete the ambiance, making guests feel calm and tranquil.

Guests will be treated to Vichy treatments performed on beautifully hand-crafted timber wet beds, especially designed in an elliptical shape to model the shape of the Q1 tower, thus connecting the two entities. For the zenith of spa rituals, Q1 Spa's signature treatment, Beyond the Big Blue, lasts a blissful four and a half hours and combines two of the spa's most rejuvenating experiences. The first, Oceam Dreaming, uses traditional Aboriginal healing techniques and includes a full body polish, ocean kelp wrap, head massage and masque and a Kodo massage and soothing foot session. A Thalasso therapy session follows, using the spa's amazing Spa jet to create a multi-sensory journey with unparalleled therapeutic benefits.

After treatments in the serenity area, the upper level of the Q1 Spa holds an unexpected treat. A stunning feature of the upper level is the glass roof which allows guests to view the spectacular skyline of the Gold Coast. With such meticulous attention paid to the Q1 Spa's design, it's no wonder the spa was voted into the 2007 Top 10 Best Spas Australasia and South Pacific by *Conde Nast Traveler*.

spa's website index

CHINA

BANYAN TREE SPA RINGHA
www.banyantreespa.com/ringha

CHI, THE SPA AT PUDONG SHANGRI-LA, SHANGHAI
www.shangri-la.com

FOREST SPRINGS, MISSION HILLS SPA, SHENZHEN
www.missionhillsgroup.com

SPRING VALLEY, MISSION HILLS SPA, SHENZHEN
www.missionhillsgroup.com

QUAN SPA, SANYA MARRIOTT RESORT & SPA
www.marriott.com/SYXMC

PLATEAU, GRAND HYATT HONG KONG
www.plateau.com.hk

THE MANDARIN SPA, HONG KONG
www.mandarinoriental.com/hongkong

TAIWAN

THE LALU SPA
www.thelalu.com.tw

JAPAN

BANYAN TREE SPA PHOENIX SEAGAIA RESORT
www.banyantreespa.com/phoenixseagaia

MANDARA SPA, ROYAL PARK SHIODOME TOWER, TOKYO
www.mandaraspa.com

MIZUKI SPA, CONRAD TOKYO
www.conradhotels1.hilton.com/en/ch/home.do

KOTORAN SPA BY CLARINS, KYOTO
www.kotoranspa.com

VIETNAM

XUAN SPA, PARK HYATT SAIGON
www.saigon.park.hyatt.com

MALDIVES

AQUUM, KURUMBA
www.peraquum.com

COMO SHAMBHALA RETREAT, COCOA ISLAND
www.cocoaisland.como.bz

SIX SENSES SPA, SONEVA FUSHI
www.sixsenses.com

ONE&ONLY SPA, ONE&ONLY REETHI RAH
www.oneandonlyresorts.com

TAJ SPA, TAJ EXOTICA RESORT & SPA, MALÉ
www.tajhotels.com

LIME, HUVAFEN FUSHI
www.limespas.com

INDIA

TAJ SPA, TAJ FISHERMAN'S COVE, CHENNAI
www.tajhotels.com

TAJ SPA, TAJ GREEN COVE RESORT, KOVALAM
www.tajhotels.com

QUAN SPA, JW MARRIOTT MUMBAI
www.marriott.com